"John Paul Lederach's vivid personal stories of his work in peacemaking illustrate his deep insights into the preeminent challenge of our times: learning how to live together in the midst of deep differences. I highly recommend this book."
—*William L. Ury, Coauthor,* Getting to Yes: Negotiating Agreement Without Giving In

"Fantastic stuff! Practical. Credible because Lederach faithfully follows the logic of Scripture and makes the words come alive in practical work in the most difficult places of the world. Hopeful concluding chapters provide additional credibility for exercising reconciliation.

"Concepts, words, methodologies, and insights flow from Lederach into the common mind. I am delighted that he possesses the rare gift of common sense and discernment. This is important material. The church needs it. The world needs it!"
—*Robert A. Seiple, Former President of World Vision*

"John Paul Lederach, experienced conciliation practitioner and teacher, reflects on the spiritual basis for peacemaking. He weaves together knowledge about conflict with biblical stories and passages, making this book helpful reading for all.

"Lederach thoughtfully and carefully listens to scriptural passages and what they have to teach us about being peacemakers and handling conflict. His fresh reading of familiar passages sheds new light on reconciliation as the center and goal of our life as Christians and the church. Lederach illustrates his claims with examples from his own experiences of international peacemaking work, including times of failure and doubt. His personal tone invites the reader into his experience and thoughts.

"This is a thoughtful and helpful book. I recommend it to those who seek understanding about the connection between conflict resolution work and Christian faith."

—*Judy Zimmerman Herr, Mennonite Central
   Committee Peace Office*

"**J**ohn Paul Lederach says that conflict opens a path to revelation and reconciliation. Each reader of this remarkable book will personally experience this prophetic insight. The dangers and horrors associated with many of the intense conflict situations with which John Paul has worked are in no way minimized. Yet he shares with us the sources of his strength for dealing with them.

"John Paul draws on the rich heritage of biblical stories, with a powerful instinct for mining the metaphors of each one. These stories open up a new understanding of the value of that biblical heritage for a highly secularized modern world.

"The power of this book lies in the way he sees simple everyday conflicts in family and community as part of the complex web of larger conflicts, without oversimplifying serious large-scale conflicts or overdramatizing local ones. John Paul is forever a learner in every situation, and he conveys the excitement of that learning, whether the lessons come from powerful political figures or struggling farmers.

"John Paul has a special gift for teaching through paradox. By the time he has shown the inseparability of truth, mercy, justice, and peace, we understand why we can dare to hope. No one who labors in the field of peacemaking can afford to be without this book. John Paul's writing takes us both deeply into ourselves and far out to the workings of the world in which we live. Thank you, John Paul!"

—*Elise Boulding, Quaker, Professor Emerita of Sociology
   at Dartmouth College, and Former Secretary General
   of the International Peace Research Association*

THE JOURNEY TOWARD RECONCILIATION

THE
JOURNEY
TOWARD
RECONCILIATION

JOHN PAUL LEDERACH

FOREWORD BY
HAROLD H. SAUNDERS

Herald
Press

Scottdale, Pennsylvania
Waterloo, Ontario

Library of Congress Cataloging-in-Publication Data
Lederach, John Paul.
  The journey toward reconciliation / John Paul Lederach.
     p. cm.
  Includes bibliographical references.
  ISBN 0-8361-9082-3 (alk. paper)
     1. Conflict management—Religious aspects—Christianity.
  2. Conflict management—Religious aspects—Mennonites.
  3. Lederach, John Paul. 4. Religion and justice. I. Title.
  BV4597.53.C58L45   1999
  261.8'3—dc21   98-31845

The paper used in this publication is recycled and meets the minimum requirements of the American National Standard for Information Sciences—Permanence of Paper for Printed Library Materials, ANSI Z39.48-1984.

A version of chapter 2 was earlier published by *Christianity Today.* All Scripture is used by permission, all rights reserved, and unless otherwise indicated is from the *New Revised Standard Version Bible,* copyright 1989, by the Division of Christian Education of the National Council of the Churches of Christ in the USA. Scripture marked RSV is from the *Revised Standard Version Bible*, copyright 1946, 1952, 1971, by the same publisher as for NRSV; KJV, from the *King James Version of the Holy Bible;* NEB, from *The New English Bible,* © The Delegates of the Oxford University Press and the Syndics of the Cambridge University Press, 1961, 1970.

THE JOURNEY TOWARD RECONCILIATION
Copyright © 1999 by Herald Press, Scottdale, Pa. 15683
     Published simultaneously in Canada by Herald Press,
     Waterloo, Ont. N2L 6H7. All rights reserved
Library of Congress Catalog Card Number: 98-31845
International Standard Book Number: 0-8361-9082-3
Printed in the United States of America
Book and cover illustration and design by Gwen M. Stamm

08 07 06 05 04 03 02 10 9 8 7 6 5 4 3

To order or request information, please call
1-800-759-4447 (individuals); 1-800-245-7894 (trade).
Website: www.mph.org

Through Christ,
God has claimed us as friends
and granted us peace.
God has given us the ministry
of reconciliation.
—*Paul*

We all want peace.
We, we who are bearers of the good news,
have been given the ministry
of reconciliation.
It is our job, our responsibility.
—*Pedrito*

CONTENTS

An author's name in parentheses identifies a resource in the Bibliography under that name.

A PERSONAL FOREWORD

John Paul has written a deeply perceptive and practical reflection on the dynamics of the peace process. He has rooted that reflection in his own spiritual journey toward reconciliation in the company of many who suffer in conflict. His struggles with the complexities and ambiguities of that journey make the peace process intensely human—as it must be.

For three reasons, the idea of *a peace process* deserves to become the conceptual framework for the field of conflict prevention, management, and resolution.

First, it is the only conceptual framework large enough to embrace whole human beings in whole bodies politic. Peacemaking must happen at all levels of a body politic.

Of course, government officials and others with power must be involved—a point that John Paul himself acknowledges he has not fully come to terms with. There are some things only governments can do, such as negotiate, enforce, and provide resources for binding agreements.

However, there are other very important things that only citizens outside government can do, such as changing human relationships. That is why we must think of a multilevel peace process that also includes quasi-official organizations as well as the reconciling work that John Paul and others do among nonofficial groups—

what I call the "public peace process." Finally, citizens must spread and embed their experience of reconciliation through the habitual interactions of the civil society, so that this way of treating one another becomes natural.

As we flew on the diplomatic shuttles of Secretary of State Henry Kissinger after the 1973 Arab-Israeli War, we began calling our work the "negotiating process." Our strategy was to build one mediated Arab-Israeli agreement on another. Our purpose was to change the sense of possibility, to make possible tomorrow steps toward peace that were not possible yesterday, and to transform relationships however glacially in a gathering momentum toward reconciliation. That total "peace process," as we termed it, was larger than intergovernmental negotiation.

Second, peacemaking is a process, a way of living and working. Peace is never made; it is always in the making.

I see the peace process as an open-ended, multilevel political process of continuous interaction between whole groups and whole bodies politic. This means interaction across permeable borders to change relationships. John Paul more eloquently calls it a "journey toward reconciliation."

The point is that the medium for transforming hostile relationships is an evolving complex of simultaneous interactions among people at many levels of society. Such transformation happens through experience; it is not negotiated.

After leaving government, I reflected that the Arab-Israeli peace process was a series of mediated agreements embedded in a larger political process. In that continuously changing complex of human interactions, relationships slowly changed.

Third, peace is a spiritual and theological as well as a juridical concept. Negotiated agreements alone do not make peace; people do.

Concentration on changing relationships is the heart of John Paul's book. His reflections on reconciliation, both as a real-world struggle between and within people and as a struggle within his own religious tradition, deepen the humanity of the peace process. He awakens the human capacity for change.

I urge you to read John Paul's spiritual journey as a dialogue with us. His words reach well beyond those of his own Anabaptist tradition, to whom they are initially addressed.

We commit ourselves to the journey toward reconciliation because we believe it is right—even when we are not sure, as John Paul says, how it will progress or end. We believe that walking down the path to peace offers a way better than violence and an instrument more powerful than force to conduct the affairs of humankind. We pray that others will join us.

—Harold H. Saunders
  Assistant Secretary of State
    at the Camp David Summit, 1978
  Director of International Affairs, Kettering Foundation

PREFACE

In the past decade, I have had the opportunity of working extensively in many different settings around our globe, much of the time in situations experiencing war and conflict. I am often reminded of the classic book by Chinua Achebe (1988).

Achebe chose the title *Things Fall Apart* to depict the monumental changes experienced by his native Nigeria in the early decades of this century. It feels as though all of us are living in a time when so many things are falling apart—from the breaking up of nation-states to increased levels of ethnic and religious conflict.

Each morning, I am almost fearful of opening the newspaper to find out what happened the night before. With these realities around us, it takes a blind eye or crass nerves to write about reconciliation. Maybe it takes faith and hope.

In speaking about my work in conciliation and peacebuilding, I have struggled with knowing how to convey the challenges and rewards. I also want to show the theological underpinnings that sustain involvement in such endeavors. Before I spoke at one meeting, my daughter, Angie, gave me the most solid piece of advice I had received in some time: "Daddy, just tell stories and forget the rest!"

In this book I look at the real-life challenges and understandings of reconciliation in our world today. I want to flesh that out through the experiences and words of stories.

Stories are different from definitions, exegeses, or theoretical explanations. They can take on the qualities of a person, someone we interact with and learn from, someone we struggle and disagree with, someone who affirms and challenges us. Stories engulf both our hearts and minds. We talk a lot about stories in mediation and the work of conflict transformation. We believe in the need to tell and hear stories. We work to create a space that honors the experience shared in people's stories.

As a mediator working in extremely difficult, painful, and often-violent settings, I have found that stories are like a soul mate with whom we travel. At times we bump into each other; mostly we walk side by side. I can turn to the story, even stories told over and over again, and find insight, feeling, challenge, and solace. In stories I find myself. In stories I find a connection with others.

Conflict is also like a journey. We talk about getting ourselves "in" and "out" of messes, problems, and "situations." We try to figure out "where we are" on an issue, or where somebody "is headed" with a crazy idea. Our language talks about a journey. In conflict, more than in any other human experience, we see ourselves and others in new and profound ways, and we seek to restore truth and love in ourselves. If we take care to look beyond the words and the issues, we see God.

Deep conflicts are stressful and painful. At worst, they are violent and destructive. Yet at the same time, they create some of the most intense spiritual encounters we experience. Conflict opens a path, a holy path, toward revelation and reconciliation.

This book is about my experiences and ideas in trying

to walk down that holy path. These are stories from my journey toward reconciliation. I will share stories that I have heard and experienced, and from which I continue to gain new insight with each retelling. The stories are a window for looking into conflict and reconciliation.

My personal story is that of a believer, a peacemaker and mediator, a sociologist, a teacher, and always a learner. Here I do not pretend to develop a well-honed sociological theory of reconciliation nor a how-to guide for handling conflicts. I am after something different. I want to explore the spiritual foundations that undergird my work as a peacebuilding professional and academic. I want to test with you how I see the challenges of my work and the faith dimensions that motivate and sustain me.

I have chosen to write with my own Anabaptist community as a primary audience. These people of faith have given me a peacemaking heritage and a compass for my journey. I am accountable to them. Some of my stories and ideas will connect and encourage, and some will challenge and push the parameters of our practice and belief.

I therefore write with Anabaptists first in mind. The ideas, stories, and reflections will also resonate with a broad range of people who feel the call and interest in faith-based approaches to conflict transformation and peacebuilding. My objective is to be transparent about my convictions and also to engage in a dialogue across faith traditions.

In chapter 1, the story about Jacob and Esau sets the motif of a journey toward the face of God. I have divided the rest of the book into three parts. First, I open up the issues with storytelling that emerges from my own personal journey, learnings, and experiences with conflict and reconciliation. Each chapter reflects some aspect of reconciliation that I have encountered in my day-to-day work. My purpose is to share some of the complexity and at the same time the gentle enriching power of the journey toward reconciliation.

The second part explores biblical stories of conflict. As I say toward the end of chapter 7, my purpose in this section is to inquire into and develop a biblically based theology of conflict. In chapters 7-10, I share insights into how conflict works, how we can envision our responses, and how spiritual growth can be shaped and encouraged through conflict. I consider the deeper possibility that God moves with us through these most-difficult experiences.

In the third part, I offer thoughts about understanding reconciliation as a mission and a challenge. God calls people of faith to a ministry of reconciliation as we follow the Shepherd, who leads with a rod and staff.

If we are to take up such a mission, we must dream boldly and at the same time respond with an enthusiastic pragmatism that makes the dream a reality. We face the challenge of aligning ourselves with the central vision of God's reconciling presence and work throughout human history.

—John Paul Lederach
Eastern Mennonite University
Harrisonburg, Virginia

1

THE JOURNEY TOWARD
THE FACE OF GOD

Many Bible stories have shaped my thinking and practice in conflict transformation. In part 2, I will explore texts from Genesis 1, Matthew 18, and Acts 15. These are windows into a theology of conflict and reconciliation.

As a starting point, however, the story of Esau and Jacob has especially shaped the way I understand and look at reconciliation. It has provided me with a guiding framework for the other stories and ideas that I will explore. Let me start with the narrative in Genesis, chapters 25–33.

Esau and Jacob are brothers, sons of Isaac and Rebekah. Esau is the firstborn, the hunter, and the pride of his father's eyes. Jacob stays near home and close to his mother. When Isaac is old and nearly blind, he calls Esau to bless him as the firstborn son.

Esau sets out to hunt for game to roast as the meal preceding that generational blessing. While he is gone, Rebekah shows Jacob how to trick the old man into believing *he* is Esau. Not knowing and not seeing, Isaac bestows the revered blessing on his younger son, Jacob.

When Esau returns and brings the meal to his father, they both discover that they have been tricked. Esau moans with an "exceedingly great and bitter cry." He implores his father three times, "Bless me, me also, father. Have you not reserved a blessing for me? Have you only one blessing, father? Bless me, me also, father!"

(from 27:34-38). But there is nothing further that Isaac can give. He has already released the blessing for the firstborn; like an arrow in flight, it cannot be recalled. Jacob has stolen Esau's birthright and his blessing.

Esau then shouts with a voice that carries out across the tent village, "I hate Jacob! I will kill my brother!" These are the last words we hear from Esau until the brothers meet years later. On hearing this threat, Jacob flees in fear. The brothers are bitter enemies.

For many years they live separately. They have families and become wealthy. When Jacob faces difficulties with his wives' brothers, he hears the Lord say, "Return to the land of your ancestors and to your kindred, and I will be with you" (31:3). He is to return to the land where Esau lives.

Jacob *turns his face* toward Esau and the land of Seir. And he is afraid.

As he progresses on his journey, he sends messengers with gifts to appease his brother. They return saying that Esau, hearing that Jacob is coming, has set out to meet him with four hundred men.

Jacob becomes greatly distressed. He cries out to God: "Deliver me from the hand of my brother, from the hand of Esau, for I am *afraid* of him. He may come and *kill us all*, the mothers with the children" (32:11, adapted). But Jacob continues the journey toward Esau, sending gifts ahead each day as he travels.

The night before Jacob meets Esau, he comes to a ford in the stream Jabbok. He sends his wives, children, and everything he has across the stream and stays behind, alone. During the night a man comes and wrestles with him until daybreak. When the man sees that he cannot overcome Jacob, he strikes Jacob's hip out of joint and demands to be let go. But Jacob will not let him go until he gives Jacob a blessing. The man then blesses him and gives him a new name, Israel. Jacob says, "I have seen the *face of God,* and yet my life is preserved." He names the place Peniel, "The face of God," so it will be remembered (32:22-30).

The next morning Jacob rises to meet Esau. After he crosses the stream, he sees Esau coming with four hundred men. He arranges his family behind him. Turning toward his brother, Jacob bows to the ground seven times as he approaches Esau. But Esau runs to meet him, embraces him, falls on his neck, and kisses him. And they weep (33:1-4).

"What do you mean by sending me all these things?" Esau asks.

"I wanted to find your favor," Jacob replies.

"I have enough," Esau declares.

"No, please; . . . accept my present from my hand," Jacob says, "for truly to see *your face* is like seeing *the face of God*—since you have received me with such favor" (33:10).

Then after several days together, the brothers separate again. Each chooses a different valley, and they move apart.

This certainly is an amazing story of conflict and reconciliation. It leads through a metaphorical moment, "I have seen the face of God." It moves on to a powerful similitude, or point of comparison: "to see your face is like seeing the face of God."

When we read such narratives in the Bible, we too often lose track of the genuine human qualities. We tend to see the stories as sacred and removed from our own reality. But look closely. We can see and feel the real human nature woven into the telling. What I find most intriguing are the parts left untold in the story. We must explore them in our search for understanding the processes of reconciliation.

We find two brothers, one who tricks the other. We feel the depth of Esau's pain in the deception. He cries time and again for his father to bless him. His cry turns to bitter hatred. We see Jacob flee in fear. His deceptive actions will haunt him. The brothers move apart both physically and emotionally.

Here we ponder profound questions about conflict and reconciliation. How and when do we surface and address the injustice that was committed? How and in what ways is putting distance between persons, moving apart, a necessary part of the journey toward reconciliation? How do we respond to people who are at this point in their journey? The pain is so deep, the injustice so clear and immediately present, and the emotions so high! Is it legitimate to separate?

Such a view of reconciliation means we must be cautious about quick formulas of "forgiveness" and being "nice" to each other. Well-intentioned people may advise estranged parties to quickly forgive and forget. Yet those parties may need a long time and geographical separation for healing to occur. As in the case of these two brothers, the separation might last for decades.

One of the least-understood aspects of reconciliation is how to think about and allow for spaces of separation as an acceptable stage in the spiritual journey toward reconciliation. At these times, we *wonder* and *wander*. We are perplexed, awestruck by events, and groping for direction. Where is justice? Why me? Where is God?

Years later, the Lord asks Jacob to return, to take the

journey back to Esau. We hear Jacob's cry: "I am afraid. My brother, my sworn enemy, may kill me and my entire family."

Behind Jacob's cry is the voice we all have felt and the question we all have asked: *How can I journey toward that which threatens my life and creates in me the greatest fear?* The biblical account does not give us a detailed explanation. We are missing information at perhaps the most crucial point.

Jacob's earlier journey took him away from Esau, and now he turns his face back toward the thing that scares him the most. What makes this *turn* possible? Is it his life experiences and maturity? Has he suffered injustice? Is it uniquely divine intervention? If that is the case, how do we hear God when all of our human senses are telling us the opposite?

How can people who work for reconciliation help create conditions where this sort of turning is possible? How can we accompany those who are in a long process of turning?

I have learned that there is no magic formula or technique we can apply to create the turn. The mystery of reconciliation is the most significant aspect of the journey. *The turn* is not something we can humanly produce or control.

We follow Jacob's journey of fear and struggle back to Esau. He moves toward that fear in a journey that will ultimately involve a struggle with himself and with God. He walks to meet his enemy. We are given no explanation for Esau's journey or window into it. We follow Jacob, who is guilty of manipulation, lying, and wrongdoing.

A few clues along the way tell us how Jacob's journey

proceeds. Nothing tells how Esau moves through his bitter anger, how he turns toward his offender and oppressor, and then embraces him as a long-missed brother. What makes such grace possible? Is it Jacob's visible repentance? How can Esau be sure that Jacob's repentance is not another manipulation? How would Esau have responded if Jacob had not repented?

What if Esau had not fared well over the years and the outcome of the injustice was a life of misery for him? How do we accompany the many Esaus in their journeys toward and through bitter anger and injustice and ultimately toward their oppressors? How do we accompany Jacob on his journey toward self-understanding, facing his fear, and returning to his enemy?

We feel the intense emotion when the brothers meet. In great fear, Jacob finds a brother who embraces him. Esau finds a lost brother. They weep with each other. Several important signposts in this story provide me with a way to understand the complex scenery that marks the landscape of reconciliation. I will return to these signposts frequently.

Reconciliation as a Journey

The primary metaphor in the story of Esau and Jacob is setting out on a *journey*. In the first journey, the brothers separate, moving away from each other. For Jacob, the journey of separation is driven by fear and perhaps a deep inner sense of guilt that cannot be faced. For Esau, it seems driven by bitterness and hatred, rooted in a profound experience of injustice.

We are not told in detail how each overcomes what has driven them, nor how much time it takes to change. We are told something that is consistent with nearly every other story of reconciliation in the Bible. The Lord says, "Turn. Go back. Take the journey toward your enemy. I will be with you." As a journey, reconciliation is understood as both the *flight away* and the daring *trip back*.

Ultimately, reconciliation is a journey *toward* and *through* conflict. In this instance, God does not promise to do the work for Jacob. God does not promise that he will take care of everything and level the road for Jacob. God promises to accompany him, to be present.

Reconciliation as Encounters

One cannot lightly set out on the journey through conflict nor conduct it without a high cost. We see the pain and anguish in the encounters. In general, we think about reconciliation as a single encounter bound to the time and place where enemies meet face to face. Yet in the story of Esau and Jacob, there are at least three encounters during the journey. What happens is not neatly bound up in a single encounter.

Along the way, encounters happen episodically, as metaphorical moments when we notice God's truth breaking into our lives. I believe there are encounters in every journey of reconciliation. They are different, yet at points interwoven and almost indistinguishable. They are the encounters with *self*, with *God,* and with *other(s)*.

The journey through conflict toward reconciliation always involves turning to face oneself. Jacob has to face his fear. To turn toward his brother, his enemy, he first has to deal with himself, his own fears, and his past actions. In this sense, at least, we can understand the long night of fighting alone with the stranger. During that night he fights with his own past and his fears about the future, then sees the face of God.

The journey toward reconciliation is not a path for the weak and feeble. Facing oneself and one's own fears and anxieties demands an outward *and* an inward journey. Along the journey of conflict, we always encounter ourselves, and in doing so, we come face to face with God, our Maker, whose image we bear, and who calls on us to "return."

Fear and bitterness are rooted in the experiences we have had with others. The journey toward reconciliation always involves turning toward the people who have contributed to our pain. As in the case of Jacob, it means turning toward the enemy. There are two important changes during Jacob's journey. First, he *turns toward* Esau. Second, he *seeks the face* of his brother. It is impossible for us to make significant progress on the journey of reconciliation without these two elements.

We turn and begin to walk in the direction of the person we fear. When we turn, we face a new destiny. We are not moving away from a person and a place. Instead, we are moving toward a place of reconciliation. That place is the face of the enemy that we seek. The story tells of Jacob "seeing" the face of Esau. He looks for and looks into that which he has feared the most.

In both actions—to turn and to seek—I find profound challenges. The journey of reconciliation requires us to expose our faces in a way that seems enormously risky. We feel vulnerable. Yet we must turn toward what most frightens us in the depths of our souls: the face of our enemy. To seek that face is to see in our enemy a person.

As we set out on this messy and quite-human journey, we find that we encounter God. This is the paradox. When we fight all night in the darkness of our soul and

fear, we struggle with God. When we turn to seek the
face of our enemy, we look into the face of God.

This is Jacob's journey. He fights all night with the
stranger, a long night of fighting himself and his fears,
and he sees God face-to-face. The next day he is bowing
himself to the ground seven times as he approaches his
brother. Esau embraces him. Jacob exclaims, "To see
your face is like seeing the face of God."

We will find God present throughout the journey toward reconciliation, in the depths of fear, in the hopelessness of dark nights, in the tears of reconnection. We
experience dazzling insight, defining moments that
show where we are going and who we are becoming in
our relationships. The pathway through conflict toward
reconciliation is filled with God-encounters, if we have
the eyes to see, the ears to hear, and the heart to feel.

Reconciliation as a Place

This journey leads to a place. In the story of Esau and
Jacob, that place involves heartfelt reunion. We sometimes think of this as the ultimate resolution, the ending place. But we need to understand that the journey
has many places along the way. Each of the major encounters—with self, with the enemy, and with God—is
marked by a place. A *place* is a specific time and space
where certain things *come together* in the journey.

In the story of Esau and Jacob, these places are marked,
named, and memorialized. In these places people have
met their enemies, God has met people, and individuals
have encountered themselves and gained new awareness. Here again is the extraordinary dual nature of reconciliation: It is both a place we are trying to reach and
a journey we take to get there.

Usually we, as individuals and societies, mark our encounters by remembering those aspects of conflict that have produced pain, loss, and sacrifice. For example, most of our official remembrance markers refer to war, places of great loss, or important military victories. But in the story of Esau and Jacob, the altars are built and places are named to help people remember where God has encountered a person on the journey toward the enemy and reconciliation.

Once Jacob and Esau reach the place of reconciliation where they meet face-to-face, it is still not the end. The journey goes on, but the two brothers do not stay together. This story does not have a fairy-tale ending with everyone living together happily ever after. The journey leads to an encounter and a place; that encounter and place lead to new journeys. Such is the lifelong walk with self, the other, and God.

The story of Esau and Jacob leaves us with this landscape of memorialized places that celebrate metaphorical moments. Reconciliation is a journey, an encounter, and a place. God calls us to set out on this journey. It is a journey through conflict, marked by places where we see the face of God, the face of the enemy, and the face of our own self.

PART 1
STORIES
FROM THE
RECONCILIATION
ROAD

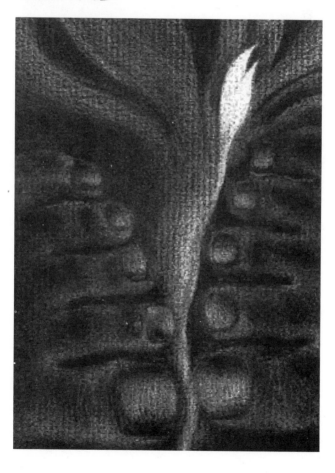

2
MY ONLY CHILD

Sometimes one event can change a person's life forever. It will stand out in the mind with a vivid clarity and immediacy even though years have passed. Such is the case with a phone call I received one evening in our home in San Jose, Costa Rica.

When the phone rang, I was lying in bed, reading a book to Angie, three years old. At the other end of the line was the familiar voice of a key Miskito leader in the armed resistance, who had been fighting against the Nicaraguan government. He had become my close friend in the past year.

"John Paul," he said, "I have some difficult news. I have been informed by a good source that there is a plan to take your daughter. They want you out."

Even as I write these words, I can still feel the shiver, the blood draining from my face, and the pounding of my heart.

"What are you talking about?" My dry mouth struggled to stammer intelligent words.

"I cannot give you details on the phone. We can talk tomorrow. But, listen, it is very serious and includes the three-letter boys," referring to the CIA (U.S. Central Intelligence Agency). "You have to tell your wife to break all her routines. Don't let them go to school tomorrow. Don't open your doors. Watch carefully."

The words seemed unreal, like a bad dream. I knew we

couldn't talk, but I could not let him go.

"Come on," I heard myself saying, "how serious is this?"

I will never forget his last words: "John Paul, now you are one of us."

I hung up the phone and went back to Angie, who seemed never to go to sleep. My mind was racing. A question kept cropping up: "What in the world have I gotten us into?"

I had gotten us into peacemaking. I was part of a team of church leaders who had been working intensely to bring together leaders of the Nicaraguan government and leaders of the east-coast resistance. The negotiations were aimed at ending the nearly eight-year war. Other more-key mediators were located inside the country, but they had difficulty traveling because of the tense relationship between Nicaragua and the rest of the region.

During the months before this phone call, I had become a communication link, often shuttling messages between opposition leaders located in Costa Rica and Sandinista officials in Managua, Nicaragua.

By the next day, with even more frightening information, we shuttled the family out of the house and the country. In the next weeks and months, I returned to Costa Rica on my own to continue the work. Eventually negotiations were arranged and a cease-fire was put in place.

In the process, those who did not want a separate Indian negotiation increased their threats and violence. During that restless night and many times since, I have often been haunted by a nagging thought: "Peace is a noble pursuit, but at what price?"

Over the years and continuing even now, I have

worked in settings of protracted conflict and wars. This work has always left me with a sense of fragility, as the story behind the phone call shows. Yet there is more than the personal side. Wars emerge for such complex reasons with so many levels of activity and consequence. These reasons arise from histories of animosity and strife between people that date back generations. They involve nations and their powerful and mixed interests.

We Anabaptists often talk of peace. Yet in real life, building international conciliation and peace is an enormously complex task. In the midst of war, we find it difficult to understand the feelings and perceptions of people involved. We want to assist and help create the space for reconciliation, uprooting the ferocious weeds of war so that peace can be planted. But that goal appears remote. Most of the time it seems to be hopeless, a utopian dream.

I am consistently faced with perplexing questions: How do we move from merely talking about peace to actually building peace? How can we promote a concern for human life and justice in settings of devastating violence and oppression? How do we bring enemies together?

I spend much of my time working with and between enemies. Frequently, in Nicaragua, Somalia, or the Philippines, I am with people who threaten others and feel threatened by others. Enemies have killed some of their friends, and they have killed enemies. They are suspicious and suspected. They have been hated, and they have hated.

As a person involved in peacebuilding, I have also become more absorbed with studying enemies. How do I work with them and between them? How can I ever accept and deal with their intense levels of fear and hatred?

From such real-life experiences and questions, I have returned to and struggled with understanding various images of enemies found in the Bible. This is a challenge before me: How to convey the complexity of reconciliation work in the context of war, while at the same time finding practical and faithful responses. I begin by telling stories about the journey with my own enemies.

This personal journey began with that crazy phone call. It was the first time that I had come face-to-face with an enemy who truly wanted to harm me and those I loved. The events of that night and the years of work since have led me to reconsider two seemingly contradictory biblical images of enemies found in the Bible: the cry to crush the enemies, and the call to love them.

Deliver Me and Crush My Enemies

For many years, my peace theology did not push me to deal with Old Testament stories of crushing the enemy. Finally this happened when I "became one of them" and entered that terrible world of paranoia and fear. I connected in a personal and vicarious way with the sentiment of crushing enemies found in the Old Testament.

Before that phone call, I had never truly felt both threat from an enemy and hatred for that enemy. After the phone call, those emotions became real. At times my inner community of little voices cried out, "Lord, who are these people? What right do they have to do this? Who in their right mind would threaten to take a three-year-old innocent child to pursue a seemingly insignificant political objective? What kind of people would do this?"

My sense of anger and injustice only increased with the knowledge that behind the threats were nameless and faceless beings. I had become the enemy of people who could hide, manipulate, and ruin lives with one stroke. For a few dollars, they could have me killed. These were people whom I would never know. I could never hold them accountable for their actions.

For the first time, in a personal way, I experienced the presence of true evil. Through these events, my heart bypassed my pacifist mind and connected with the voice of the psalmist (as in Pss. 55–58), crying, "Lord, deliver me and crush my enemies!" Listen to these powerful words:

Lord, I am distraught by the noise of the enemy,
  because of the oppression of the wicked.
    (55:2-3, RSV)

Destroy their plans, O Lord,
  Confuse their tongues. (55:9, RSV)

The wicked go astray from the womb;
  they err from their birth, speaking lies.
They have venom like the venom of a serpent. (58:3-4)

O God, break the teeth in their mouths;
  tear out the fangs of the young lions, O Lord!
Let them vanish like water that runs away;
  like grass let them be trodden down and wither.
Let them be like the snail that dissolves into slime;
  like the untimely birth that never sees the sun.
    (58:6-8)

The righteous will rejoice when they see vengeance
    done;
  they will bathe their feet in the blood of the wicked.
People will say,
  "Surely there is a reward for the righteous;
  surely there is a God who judges on earth." (58:10-11)

Rarely has a Mennonite preached on these texts!

While working in Central America, I had been close to the violence of war. I knew war and all that it brings. I knew families that had lost parents, children, brothers, and sisters. I had friends who lost limbs and even their lives. No matter how much I knew, it was only after the experiences of direct manipulation and violence *against me* that I began to understand the deep anger that accompanies fear. I learned the frustration of helplessness and the bitter taste of hatred.

In becoming "one of them," I experienced, even if in a small a dose, the deep cry for a just God and the absolute dependence on God for deliverance.

A second story is related to the first. In the months that followed, in spite of these pressures and threats, we achieved a measure of success by helping to bring leaders of the Miskito-Sandinista conflict to negotiations.

As part of the initial accords, all of the leaders agreed to go to the east coast of Nicaragua, into the home areas of the indigenous leaders. For many of the exiled leaders, this was the first time in years that they had gone back. It was the first time any of them had returned openly in the presence of former enemies.

This was a time of both expectation and vulnerability. The leaders had made some progress at the negotiating table in the formality of capital cities. However, it was difficult to carry out those agreements or even explain them in the villages where the war had raged. Our conciliation team was asked to accompany the returning leaders to meet their communities and talk about the peace process. The leaders invited us to walk with them into the heart of reconciliation and all its challenges.

It seemed like a logical proposal, but it was not an easy

task. People on both sides had questions and suspicions. We did not have the protocol and formality of negotiations in Managua hotels. In the villages, it was an organic process. People stood face-to-face with the very enemies they had sought to control, enemies who in many instances had killed members of their immediate families.

We traveled long days and hours by riverways into remote areas of the country. In some villages, people came forward for the first time to speak about difficulties faced at local levels with various leaders on both sides of the conflict. In one village, people went on at some length, detailing atrocities committed by a particular local Sandinista military leader who was present at that meeting.

In such situations where great pain and emotion are expressed, it is difficult if not impossible to control what spins out of the event. That night, the Sandinista military leader and several of his men were attacked and seriously wounded. The word rapidly spread ahead of us.

By the time we reached the main city in the northeast, the Sandinista sympathizers were up in arms against what they saw as inflammatory speeches of the returning indigenous leaders. They demanded that no further speeches be made since they created conditions ripe for violence.

Puerto Cabezas was the largest of the Miskito centers. The indigenous leaders insisted on holding a public meeting to talk about the peace process, in accord with agreements reached in the capital with top-level Sandinistas. However, the local Sandinista leaders did not approve. In some instances, they orchestrated open and violent response to the returning Indians.

As the day approached for the main event, an impasse developed. Miskito leaders said they would hold the public meeting. Sandinista leaders said they could not guarantee anyone's safety if they did.

The conciliation team literally worked day and night to stave off violence, but inevitably the situation deteriorated. The open meeting was set for noon. We decided that in tune with our work, we would accompany Indian leaders throughout the day, hoping that our presence would make violence less likely.

The day before, we had separate meals with both sides and again pleaded for restraint. In the morning before we left the house, we gathered to pray as a team. In our prayers, we named leaders and key persons on all sides, those who were friends, and those who we knew were angry and volatile.

Shortly thereafter, it became clear that a worst-case scenario was developing. The meeting was to be held in the baseball stadium. During the morning people gathered in the stadium. Soon mobs began to appear, particularly groups of Sandinista youth armed with clubs, chains, and machetes. The speakers in the public meeting could barely be heard over the din of angry voices.

As one of the Moravian pastors opened with prayer, machine guns crackled behind us, mostly as a disruption, creating confusion. When the speeches finally ended, some members of our team accompanied the Indian leaders to their houses. I stayed with Carlitos, a fellow member of the conciliation team, to bring out the pickup that had been used as a podium for the speeches.

In the streets around the stadium, hand-to-hand fighting and rioting broke out. As we were about to leave the stadium, a large group of the mob rushed inside. They entered the only exit that we had for leaving the grounds. In the chaos, a young Sandinista recruit pointed at me and shouted, "There's the gringo. Get him! Get him!"

A mental image of that moment is frozen in my memory. I can look into that crowd and see the faces of young people, some whom I knew. There was frenzy in their faces as their eyes turned and riveted on me. *I* was the foreign enemy. *I* represented the United States, the enemy they could never touch. For years that enemy had been beyond their reach. That enemy was the cause of economic hardships and oppression, and had provided weapons for their enemy. Now that enemy was within their grasp.

I represented America and all the suffering they could never escape. In their eyes I could see the years of frustration, of lost loved ones, of a pain that festers into resentment and boils up and out in an uncontrolled anger.

The rest is a blur of a few seconds. We made a leap for the truck and started the fifteen yards through the mob toward the only exit. The first thing that hit us was a logging chain, shattering the windshield and sending glass into our arms and faces. By the time we had gone a few feet, not a window was left in the truck.

I can still feel the blows of stones, a two-by-four landing on my shoulder, and the splatter of Carlitos's warm blood that hit my cheek when he was hit in the back of the head. Miraculously, he did not pass out as he drove slowly through the gauntlet of people throwing stones.

Minutes later we were in the local hospital, where we were cleaned and stitched up by a Cuban doctor. I remember sitting in that hospital waiting room, my eyes and body jerking at the sound of shouts or gunshots. My mind was racing with one thought: "Just take me to a safe place." I felt a fear that crossed over into paranoia.

In less than a year, I had faced a variety of dangers. I had been accused of being a Communist Sandinista spy. My daughter's life had been threatened. I had received multiple assassination threats. I had been called a dog of the CIA. I had been stoned.

No longer do I question the suspicious, paranoid attitudes of those in war. Now I know the craziness of a fearful mind that looks behind and thinks every person is a possible threat.

No longer do I wonder how one group could see another as a real threat to their existence. I know how it feels to be falsely accused, arrested, and interrogated.

No longer do I doubt the reality of an anger that flows into hate. I have experienced such anger from my own heart, and I have been the object of such hatred.

When I hear those powerful, almost embittered words from the psalmist, I no longer dismiss them. Instead, in so many circumstances around our globe, I am drawn to the cry that flows from the angry heart. I have come to believe much more deeply in the proper place of righteous indignation.

In too many places around our globe, I have felt and seen the rushing white-water rapids pounding out the psalmist's cry. I am convinced that reconciliation has a home in that river of pain, with those who seek deliverance and justice.

The Love of God
Inside these experiences with real enemies, I also heard another voice. It was the voice of God's search for reconciliation as a call to love those who do us harm.

As I write this, I am working with Angie's Sunday school class some six years after the events I just described. This week their assignment is to memorize John 3:16: "For God so loved the world that he gave his only Son, so that everyone who believes in him may not perish but have eternal life."

This most-popular verse has taken on a whole new meaning for me since our time in Central America and my work these past years in the context of wars. We have traditionally understood John 3:16 as a creedal formula. We tend to place the emphasis on the part that says, "Everyone who believes in him may . . . have eternal life." What counts, in terms of faith, is the belief.

However, look again. Embedded in the verse is a story of a parent who gave up a child. As parents who have had our only child threatened, this story is all too real. I have never experienced anything so precious as the gift of our firstborn, Angie, and her younger brother, Joshua. Even with all the challenges, the energy, the sleepless nights, and the sibling fights—nothing matches the gift of a life placed in our hands for nurture, love, and growth.

This is why the phone call shook me awake and made me see things differently. I was faced with the reality of ultimate sacrifice. When I said I could feel the blood drain from my face as I listened to the words from the phone that night, I meant it literally. I felt an immense internal sense of my heart being crushed.

I could face a threat against me, but how could I face a threat to my only child? What activity could be worth the cost of losing my daughter? Was pursuing peace in Nicaragua worth the life of my child? Think about it. Is there anything that is so important to you that you would give up your child to achieve it?

With this thought in mind, let us turn our attention to John 3:16. This sacrificial choice is at the heart of

God's search for reconciliation. As a father and a human being, I find it incomprehensible that God, as a parent, gave up this most precious gift to reconcile erring and belligerent enemies with himself.

I can understand sacrifice for family or friends. For example, I would not hesitate to give a risky blood transfusion, or endanger my life if it meant saving the life of my child. However, to do this *for enemies* is beyond understanding.

I can no longer take John 3:16 as a short formula for salvation. I can only understand it as a foundational principle of reconciliation. It is an ethic based on willingness to make the ultimate sacrifice on behalf of an enemy. It is an ethic undergirded by and made possible only through the immeasurable love and grace of God.

As the hymn exclaims, "O love of God, how rich and pure! How measureless and strong! It shall forever more endure, the saints' and angels' song" (Lehman). It is a love like that described by the apostle Paul. He declared, "Neither death, nor life, nor angels, nor rulers, nor things present, nor things to come, nor powers, nor height, nor depth, nor anything else in all creation, will be able to separate us from the love of God in Christ Jesus our Lord" (Rom. 8:38-39).

I have experienced that love in many ways, from the protection of our family in Central America to grace that covers a multitude of shortcomings. I aspire to bring this love to the world, but I recognize that I barely understand its real height or depth. Time and again, I find that I fall short. I am much less able to practice and live by it fully. I only know that this love ultimately sustains life and is the essence of God's very nature, the God who seeks reconciliation with the enemy through self-sacrifice.

Conclusion

As a peacebuilder, I have struggled with real-life experiences and with the biblical images of enemies. A few points important in my learnings may contribute to developing a practical theology of the enemy as part of a theology of reconciliation.

First, I am surprised by the obvious. Enemies are present throughout the faith story. Without enemies, the story of reconciliation and faith itself cannot be told. As pacifists, we cannot develop theologies of easy peace accomplished through promises of humanistic love. There is nothing human about loving one's enemy. Living faithfully in the face of enemies is only possible with a deep spiritual connection to God's love and a willingness to live as vulnerably as Jesus did.

In this regard, I am struck again by the story of Jacob and Esau's encounter. As their story develops, Jacob is fearful of his brother's rage. His brother has become his worst enemy. On the last night of the journey toward his brother, Jacob fights all night with God in person. Afterward Jacob says, "I have seen God face to face" (Gen. 32:30).

The next morning, Jacob humbles himself before his feared enemy, Esau, only to discover the emotional release of reconciliation. He exclaims to his brother, the former enemy, "To see your face is like seeing the face of God" (33:10). This is the journey of reconciliation, a journey where we struggle directly with God and ultimately seek the face of God in the enemy.

Second, in pursuit of reconciliation, we must also deal with the extraordinary and paradoxical biblical images of enemies. A theology of the enemy must integrate two kinds of agony. We must truly hear and honor the cry for deliverance, and also acknowledge and give legitimate place to anger.

I have concluded that effective peacebuilders often emerge from two different sources. One source is angry pacifists who have touched the river of human pain and translate their heartfelt cries into specific action. Another source is people who from oppression and frustration sought solution in violence. At some point they stepped beyond violence to embrace the journey of personal and social healing, even reaching out to their enemies.

In both instances, anger was translated into a vision of reconciliation. From my experience, I have come to a strong realization: I cannot face the enemy unless I am rooted in God's sustaining love and at the same time give myself permission to struggle with the seemingly impossible sacrifice it represents. To pursue reconciliation, we must accept the long sleepless night of fighting in ourselves with God before we can journey toward and look for the face of God in our enemy.

In this personal story that began with the phone call, I found that developing a theology of the enemy poses a challenge. In the cry for deliverance, how can we make room to acknowledge the rightful place of anger? At the same time, how can we embrace God's sacrificial, unending love and live by that love? Eventually, the journey toward reconciliation always leads us to seek the face of the enemy and the face of God.

3
THE COLONEL

The Colonel seemed to explode out of his clothes.
Unspoken words rolled across my tongue,
leaving again the raw taste of righteous disdain.
"Whose life today, Colonel?"
The image danced on my mind's stage.

This fragment comes from a poem I have been writing about my experience with the colonel. I say I "have been writing" because I never get it quite right. I have tried to tell the story of the colonel only one time in a public meeting. I broke down into such tears that I could barely finish.

I do not have a logical explanation for the emotion. When I tell stories of my experiences with reconciliation, I easily become emotional, even when I've told the story many times.

I was encouraged and challenged by the words of K. M. George, writing with Orthodox perspectives on Christian spirituality (George). He notes that in much of Western society and Christianity, tears have been ignored and relegated to an insignificant place. In the tradition of Orthodox leaders in the early church, tears are part of "becoming prayer," signs of compassion. I wish that were my case.

At times I feel that my tears are more the signs of pent-up emotion arising from intense experience. My tears for the colonel, I believe, were perhaps because I had an overwhelming awareness of my weakness and hypocrisy. God spoke to me through the colonel, and I was humbled.

Encountering an Epiphany

Early in 1987, I was traveling in Honduras near the border with Nicaragua. The Contra war was still raging. Along this border, particularly in the outskirts of the remote village of Danli, Honduran Mennonite brothers and sisters had been displaced from their homes. This happened because Nicaraguan resistance troops occupied the region as their military base. They were opposing the Sandinista government. Some Hondurans hailed the troops as freedom fighters, and others counted them as counter-revolutionaries.

At that time, the Honduran government claimed there were no Nicaraguan fighters based in Honduras. It was a hidden war of great cost. I had traveled with Carmen and Luke Schrock-Hurst, who were working with the displaced families. These people had the pain of lost time, homes, and family members etched in their faces. They were victims in a war for freedom that was not theirs.

After that trip, I stood at the large plate-glass window and was looking out over the airport tarmac at Tegucigalpa, the capital of Honduras. There I first saw the colonel. I had checked in two hours early and was alone in the departure room, absorbed in my thoughts about the day's travels.

The words of the young Honduran mother ran through my mind. "Nonexistent soldiers" occupied her family's house. "How do you take it?" I had asked, expecting some bitterness. Her answer surprised me: "I feel pain for them. They are so young. They have so little hope. They know only death."

I was trying to sort through her experience, which I could barely understand, when the sirens in the airport went off. There was instant action. Soldiers hustled across the runway to a fleet of helicopters, which slowly rose and filed off toward the mountains bordering Nicaragua. From my spot at the window, I could see it all. *Is this a drill or the real thing?* I wondered.

The helicopters would quickly arrive at the areas I had just traveled, probably to support Contra fighters. A little less than an hour later, the helicopters started flying back. One by one they came over the crest of the hill, flying low, floating a few feet above the ground. One of the war birds peeled off and came directly toward the terminal. The wind from its rotor slammed the door shut a few feet from where I stood. The noise was deafening.

The chopper settled down a few yards from the window, so close that I could see the pilot. His face was taut, his eyes hidden behind dark Ray-Bans. The side door of the helicopter flew open, and out jumped a passenger. He wore civilian clothes and carried a small duffel bag.

The passenger ran to the terminal door, joked a bit with the customs officials, and then jumped across the customs table. Just then I sat down, and he sat beside me. He was American. He did not pay taxes or show a passport or ticket.

The Honduran pilot took the helicopter to join the fleet across the runway. About an hour later, his American passenger left on a flight to San Salvador.

My Tan-Sahsa flight was late arriving from New Orleans. I waited and watched as people slowly filled up the seats around me. A truck pulled up past the window, and a Honduran military official stepped out. He was dressed in a green fatigue jumpsuit, black boots, and dark glasses. The official walked right past the window, and I recognized him as the pilot of the helicopter I had seen earlier. He was a big man, well muscled, almost exploding out of his suit.

A perfect Rambo! I thought. *Who is this man? Does he really believe in what he is doing? What did he just do on the border, this very afternoon? Whose lives did he take?* My mind was racing with the images I had just seen in Danli.

As he entered, customs officials smiled and called him *"mi Coronel."* He spoke briefly with them, then went back out the door. There he stood, waiting for the flight to arrive from the United States, the same one that I would take to Costa Rica.

Within minutes that plane pulled up to the terminal. As we waited to board, the arriving passengers filed past the window on their way to the immigration and customs room. The colonel was waiting for someone on that flight.

This should be interesting, I thought. *Who are you picking up this time, mi Coronel? What mercenary for freedom will you escort this time?* A righteous disdain floated in my pacifist mind as I positioned myself to get a better look at the coming encounter. *What secrets are held in your mind? Who are your contacts? Is this not the very evil of the war itself? American and Honduran militaries ganging up against oppressed Nicaraguans!*

The colonel moved toward the plane to meet his friend and disappeared from my sight. A few minutes later, he reappeared. His arm was around a ten-year-old girl. Metal braces supported her thin legs. She was smiling and waving and trying to walk all at once.

The muscular body of the colonel seemed engulfed by her enthusiasm. He tried to find a way to help her. First he tried to take her hand and then awkwardly put his arm behind her to support her back.

They slowly made their way past my window. His Ray-Ban glasses were off. For a moment he looked through the window at me, and our eyes met. What I saw startled me. *The colonel is a father like me!* It was a metaphorical moment of stunning insight.

To this day, I carry that image of the colonel with me. I still try to understand and learn from what happened in those moments. I never spoke with the colonel. I never shook his hand. I do not know who he was or what involvement he had in the war. But I do know that in the space of a short time, I had created the image of an enemy.

Creating Enemies

In thinking about my own process, I have concluded that enemies are created. Lay aside all the other factors, from social conditioning to real physical threat. In the end, an enemy is rooted and constructed in our hearts and minds and takes on social significance as others share in the construction. From my own experience, I have learned that critical steps need to be taken to construct an enemy. Each step is in the story of the colonel.

First, to construct an image of the enemy, I must *separate* myself from another. In my mind and rooted in my heart, I begin to see in another person, not the sameness we share, but the differences between us that I identify as negative. I attach to those differences a negative judgment, a projection that this person is a threat to me and is wrong.

Inside, hidden, unexplored, and unrecognized, is a question about myself, who I am, and what I believe. In a subtle but critical way, the enemy is connected to my own self-view and identity. Who I am is defined by who I am not. The origin of enmity lies in a self-definition built on a negative projection about another. I imagine that the other person is completely bad and that I am completely good.

A second phenomenon goes hand in hand with separation. I see myself as *superior.* Superiority is the qualitative opposite of what we see in the example of Jesus emptying himself (Phil. 2:7). Jesus, though in the form of God, did not regard his position as superior. Instead, he humbled himself to take the form of a common person, even a slave. In other words, he sought to bring compassion by being like others. He recognized and embraced his sameness. He chose to take his place as a servant.

When I feel superior, I believe I am not only different from but better than the other person. It is the incarnation story in reverse. Though I am in the form of a common person, the same as others, I raise myself above them and take the position of God. To construct an enemy, we must both lose sight of our sameness and create a sense that we are superior.

Third, separation and superiority lead to *dehumanizing* the other person(s). I dehumanize when I deprive people of the qualities that make them humans. I rob them of being created in the image of God. I lose the sight of God in their faces. I no longer see "that of God" in them (see chapter 8). To construct an enemy, I must both dehumanize the other and deface the image of God in that person.

What I did in a matter of minutes with the colonel

carried these elements and dynamics. I separated myself from him. I saw myself as morally superior. I felt a certain righteousness about myself. I saw myself as good. I saw him as evil. My own identity as a pacifist and peacemaker became more impermeable to the degree that I cast him as my opposite, a militarist and war-maker. He was less than I was. Morally, I stood above him.

What shook my very foundation was the unexpected re-entry of human sameness and God. I saw myself in the colonel. I was shaken by this surprise from God: the colonel and I were so much alike.

In the second chapter, I said that a theology of the enemy must face the dilemma of embracing the righteous cry for justice and incarnating the sacrificial love of God.

Here is another paradox of reconciliation. We must learn how to develop a positive identity of self and group that is not based on criticizing or feeling superior to another person or group.

In Christian circles we claim to hate the sin but love the sinner (cf. Jude 23). I believe this is much more complex than it appears on the surface. It is filled with intricate trappings of self-deception and superiority. I have found it more honest within myself to say, "Be careful about what you hate. You may find that like a blindfold it removes your ability to see. Look first for what you see of yourself in others. Love the sinners, and see yourself in them. There you will find God."

My encounter with the colonel was an internal holy ground, a place I have marked on my journey toward reconciliation. That day outside the Tegucigalpa airport, God was in the burning bush. The encounter still has the power to shake me. It represents one of the things I find most scary about my work.

I have lived and talked with people who have been both victims of violence and creators of violence. I have shaken the hands of convicted terrorists and people who have tortured others. I have sat with warlords who seem merciless in their pursuit of power. I have listened to freedom fighters who cry out against injustice and pick up weapons to defend their cause. What scares me the most is not how different I am, but rather how I can see and feel a bit of myself in each of them.

Every time I come away with the reminder of the colonel in my mind and with the search to find God present in everyone. It may seem easy to understand, but I find it hard to practice. Nonetheless, this is my belief: I cannot create an enemy when I look for and find that of God in another.

This is a short chapter on a complex subject. However, writing about my personal journey toward reconciliation would be incomplete without this story. In the search to build peace, I set out to bring enemies together and to practice peace and reconciliation. The encounter with the colonel reminds me of a hard lesson. I am capable of quickly and easily creating enemies.

4
THE MEETING PLACE

During the latter half of the 1980s, much of my work was concentrated on supporting the Conciliation Team efforts for peace in Nicaragua. I worked closely with Moravian and Baptist church leaders appointed as mediators between the east-coast resistance and the Sandinista government. In chapter 2, I recounted some of the difficulties I faced.

I found this to be a time of intense learning from brothers and sisters and from the experiences we shared. I may have had more academic training in conflict resolution. However, my colleagues had waded for many years in deep waters of suffering, sharply severed relationships, and building peace in war-torn Central America.

Through the experiences, I was given many gifts: most important was a new set of lenses. For fleeting moments, I was able to see things around me in new ways. Through their eyes I saw beyond conflict resolution to reconciliation.

I saw reconciliation through the way they approached their lives and faced challenges in those years. They did not see their primary task to be resolving particular issues or applying a certain model of negotiation to the talks. They always envisioned themselves chiefly as people embedded in a set of relationships. In most instances, these were lifelong relationships between friends who now were enemies.

What they sought first was be honest in their calling of faith and to seek what was needed in these relationships. One minute a leader could be engaged in a pastoral and supportive role, and in the next minute take an exhortative and prophetic stance. They held the hands of enemies and prayed with them. They arranged plane flights and planned meals. They looked after a sick child, a relative of one of the negotiators.

In the best Latin American tradition, they were more like oldest siblings taking care of family squabbles than like professional mediators negotiating a deal. Reconciliation was restoring and healing the torn-apart web of relationships.

As we traveled together, Conciliation Team members were asked to initiate and moderate many of the meetings. All the formal negotiations in Managua started with prayer and reading a biblical text. Each of the many village meetings along east-coast riverways of Nicaragua began the same way.

Psalm 85

In most of those meetings, someone read the whole of Psalm 85. Sometimes minister Andy Shogreen, head of the Moravian Provincial Board, delivered the text. Other times Dr. Gustavo Parajon, a Baptist pastor, read it. He was the head of CEPAD, Nicaragua's evangelical relief and development organization, involving ecumenical cooperation.

In this poetic verse, the psalmist beseeches the Lord, requesting restoration and mercy. The psalm appears in the context of a people who have been exiled and are seeking to return to their land and to the Lord's favor. It makes a plea for peace, righteousness, and well-being. In verse 10, four voices are called forth, creating a rich image.

Many times I heard this Psalm read in Spanish, with words that are different from English translations, though similar to the King James imagery. In the literal translation, which captured my attention, the psalmist says in Psalm 85:10,

> Truth and Mercy have met together.
> Justice and Peace have kissed.

In these two short lines are four important concepts and two powerful paradoxes. The concepts kept dancing through my mind as I watched the peace process unfold in fits and starts. For the first time, I noticed that the psalmist seems to treat the concepts as if they are alive. I could hear their voices in the war in Nicaragua. In fact, I could hear their voices in any conflict. Truth, Mercy, Justice, and Peace were no longer just ideas. They became people, and they could talk.

I started to call forth this community of four people in my training workshops on conflict resolution. First I tried a little experiment with community leaders and pastors who were working in the local Peace Commissions in Nicaragua. These inspirational peacemakers, at considerable risk to their own lives, were involved in local-level conciliation work, bringing together warring sides in the villages. They were unsung heroes, rebuilding their communities and starring in untold stories of peace.

In the workshop, I divided the leaders and pastors into four small groups designated respectively as Truth, Mercy, Justice, and Peace. I asked each group to treat the concept as a person and to ask one question: What is Truth (or Mercy, Justice, Peace) most concerned about in the midst of a conflict?

Each group would then choose a person from their group to play the part of their character. Then I interviewed each of the role-players in front of the participants. I asked them as the characters to make first-person replies.

I addressed them, "Sister Truth," or "Brother Mercy . . ." They would respond, "I am Justice, and I am concerned that . . ." In the next step, we opened a discussion and held a little mediation session between the four people.

Over the years I have repeated the exercise with many different people and contexts. It varies each time. Unique and amazingly various insights emerge from people's experiences and concerns. As a way to understand this more fully, I have written a story that can be adapted as a play or a liturgy.

The Meeting

Greatly distressed in the midst of a nasty conflict, I kept hearing voices appealing to Truth, Mercy, Justice, and Peace. The arguments and blows had gone round and round. So finally I made a proposal. "What if," I asked the people in this awful fight, "what if we invited our four friends to join us and asked them to openly discuss their views about conflict?"

Locked in their righteous stances, the people looked at me, stunned with such an absurd idea. But I pressed ahead without paying much attention. "I have seen them come and go in other fights. I could ask them to try to clear up a few things."

Nobody objected, so I brought Truth, Mercy, Justice, and Peace into our room and sat them down in front of the belligerent crowd. I addressed the four. "We want to know what concerns you each have in the midst of conflict. May we hear your views?"

Truth stood and spoke first. "I am Truth," she said. "I am like light that is cast so all may see. In times of conflict, I want to bring forward what really happened, putting it out in the open. Not the watered-down version. Not a partial recounting. My handmaidens are transparency, honesty, and clarity. I am set apart from my three colleagues here," Truth gestured toward Mercy, Justice, and Peace, "because they need me first and foremost. Without me, they cannot go forward. When I am found, I set people free."

"Sister Truth," I interjected hesitantly, not wanting to question her integrity, "you know I have been around a lot of conflict. There's one thing I'm always curious about. When I talk to one side, like these people over here, they say that you are with them. When I talk to the others, like our friends over there, they claim you are on *their* side. Yet in the middle of all this pain, you seem to come and go. Is there only one Truth?"

"There is only one Truth, but I can be experienced in many different ways. I reside within each person, yet nobody owns me."

"If discovering you is so crucial," I asked Sister Truth, "why are you so hard to find?"

She thought for a while before replying. "I can only appear where the search is genuine and authentic. I come forward only when each person shares with others what they know of me, and when each one respects the others' voices. Where I am strutted before others, like a hand puppet on a child's stage, I am abused and shattered, and I disappear."

"Of these three friends," I pointed to the three colleagues seated around her, "whom do you fear the most?"

Without hesitation she pointed to Mercy. "I fear him," she said quietly. "In his haste to heal, he covers my light and clouds my clarity. He forgets that Forgiveness is *our* child, not his alone."

Next I turned to Mercy. "I am sure you have things to say. What concerns you?"

Mercy rose slowly and said, "I am Mercy." He seemed to begin with a plea, as though he knew that he, among them all, was under tight scrutiny. "I am the new beginning. I am concerned with people and their relationships. Acceptance, compassion, and support stand with me. I know the frailty of the human condition. Who among them is perfect?"

He turned to Truth and continued, with his eyes on her. "She knows that her light can bring clarity, but too often it blinds and burns. What freedom is there without life and relationship? Forgiveness is indeed our child, but not when people are arrogantly clubbed into humiliation and agony with their imperfections and weaknesses. Our child Forgiveness was birthed to provide healing."

I could not resist posing an urgent question: "But, Brother Mercy, in your rush to accept, support, and move ahead, do you not abort the child?"

He reacted quickly: "I do not cover Truth's light. You must understand. I am Mercy. I am built of steadfast love that supports life itself. It is my purpose in life to bring forward the eternal grace of new beginnings."

"And whom do you fear the most?" I asked.

Mercy turned, faced Justice, and spoke clearly: "My Brother Justice, in his haste to change and make things right, forgets that his roots lie in real people and relationships."

"So, Brother Justice," I said, "what do you have to say?"

"I am Justice," he responded as he rose to his feet. His strong voice was accompanied by a deep smile. "Mercy is correct. I am concerned about making things right. I consider myself a person who looks beneath the surface and behind the issues about which people seem to fight. The roots of most conflicts are tangled in inequality, greed, and wrongdoing.

"I stand with Truth, who sheds her light to expose the paths of wrongdoing. My task is to make sure that something is done to repair the damage wreaked, especially on the victims and the downtrodden. We must restore the relationship, but never while failing to acknowledge and rectify what broke the relationship in the first place."

A question chewed at my mind, and I had to ask it: "But, Brother Justice, everybody in this room feels they have been wronged. Most are willing to justify their actions, even violent deeds, as doing your bidding. Is this not true?"

"It is indeed," Justice responded. "Most do not understand." He paused as he thought for a minute.

"You see, I am most concerned about accountability. Often we think that anything and everything is acceptable. True and committed relationships have honest accounting and steadfast love. Love without accountability is nothing but words. Love with accountability is changed behavior and action. This is the real meaning of restoration. My purpose is to bring action and accountability to the words."

"Then whom do you fear?" I inquired.

"My children," he chuckled, remembering years of experience. "I fear that my children, Mercy and Peace, see themselves as parents." His voice carried a hint of gentle provocation. "Yet they are actually the fruit of my labor."

Peace burst into a glowing smile. Before I could speak, she stepped forward. "I am Peace, and I agree with all three," she began. "I am the child to whom they give birth, the mother who labors to give them life, and the spouse who accompanies them on the way. I hold the community together, with the encouragement of security, respect, and well-being."

Truth and Justice began to protest. "That is precisely the problem," said Truth in a frustrated voice. "You see yourself as greater and bigger than the rest of us."

"Arrogance!" Justice pointed his finger toward Peace. "You do not place yourself where you belong. You follow us. You do not precede us."

"That is true, Brother Justice and Sister Truth," Peace responded. "I am more fully expressed through and after you both. But it is also true that without me, there is no space cleared for Truth to be heard."

Peace turned toward Justice. "And without me, there is no way to break out of the vicious cycle of accusation, bitterness, and bloodshed. You yourself, Justice, cannot be fully embodied without my presence. I am before and after. There is no other way to reach me. I myself am the way."

Silence fell for a moment.

"And who do you fear?" I asked.

"Not who, but what and when," Peace replied. "I fear manipulation. I fear the manipulation of people using Sister Truth for their own purposes. Some ignore her, some use her as a whip, some claim to own her. I fear times when Brother Justice is sacrificed for the sake of Brother Mercy. I fear the blind manipulation when some will sacrifice life itself in trying to reach the ideal of Brother Justice. When such trickery takes place, I am violated and left as an empty shell."

I focused my attention on all four. "How would it be possible for you four to meet? What would you need from each other?"

Truth looked first at Mercy. "You must slow down, Brother Mercy. Give me a chance to emerge. Our child cannot be born without the slow development in the womb of the mother."

Mercy nodded. "Shine bright, dear Sister Truth. But please take care not to blind and burn. Remember that each person is a child of God. Each is weak and needs support to grow."

Justice was eager to speak. "I have been partly reassured by the words of Sister Peace. I need a clear statement that she gives a place for accountability and action. Remember when Micah [6:8] spoke of us: 'Love Mercy and do Justice.' You, Sister Peace, must allow room for me to come forward. If not, you will be aborted."

Peace responded on the heels of his last words. "Brother Justice, our lips will meet if we recognize that we need one another. Do not let your heart of compassion fall into bitterness that rages without purpose. I will provide the soil for you to work and bear fruit."

The four were huddled in a small circle. "And what," I asked, "is this place called where you stand together?"

"This place," they responded in unison, "is *reconciliation.*"

Then suddenly and without signal, they touched hands and danced. It was as if the dance came only rarely, like the weaving of lines and bodies around a Maypole. I could hardly distinguish one from the other as they swung from the room. No one said a word. No music was in the air, only the images of the interwoven bodies of Truth, Mercy, Justice, and Peace.

Conclusion

I learned important insights about reconciliation from the Nicaraguan experience and from years of reflection and experimentation with Psalm 85. As suggested in the story of Jacob and Esau (see chap. 1), Psalm 85 reinforces the understanding that reconciliation is both a journey we must take and a place we are trying to reach.

The psalmist provides new and deeper insight into the idea that reconciliation is a *locus*, a meeting place. With these stories, we are exploring reconciliation as a place where we encounter ourselves, others, and God. Psalm 85 presents reconciliation as a dynamic social space where different but interdependent social energies and concerns are brought together and given voices.

The primary practical task of those working for reconciliation is to help create the *dynamic social space* where Truth, Mercy, Justice, and Peace can truly meet and thresh things out. We experiment with various procedures and mechanisms that serve this goal.

Too often in the midst of conflict, we take these social energies (the four sibs) as contradictory forces, voiced by different persons within the conflict. They are seen as pitted against each other. Those who cry out for Truth and Justice are taken as adversaries of those who plead for Mercy and Peace, and they often understand themselves that same way.

The vision of the psalmist is different. Reconciliation is possible only as each sees the place and need for the other. This approach means that each voice and the social energy it produces is incomplete without the other.

What does this mean at a practical level? We must pay attention and give space to the different energies represented by the voices of Truth, Mercy, Justice, and Peace. When these voices are heard as contradictory forces, we find ourselves mired in erupting conflict and paralyzed by it. We argue endlessly over which is more important, justified, or proper.

When we hear these four voices as contradictory, we are forced into a false position of choosing one or the other. It is as if they were in a boxing match that only leaves winners and losers. Such tunnel vision should not exist. We are not asked to choose between rain or sunshine. Each is different, but both are needed for sustaining life and growth. Such is the case with Truth and Mercy, Justice and Peace.

Psalm 85 shows that conflict has revelatory and reconciling potential when the four different energies are embraced. We need to recognize all their concerns as proper, provide them with voices, respond to their fears and needs, and place them in an open and dialogical setting. That is better than roping them into a boxing match, as adversaries. By letting all of them speak, they are less likely to be driven underground or to extremes. As we deal with conflict this way, God reveals the road to reconciliation.

Let us create the social space that brings Truth, Mercy, Justice, and Peace together within a conflicted group or setting. Then energies are crystallized that create deeper understanding and unexpected new paths, leading toward restoration and reconciliation.

5
TIME, HEALING, AND RECONCILIATION

We need time. I frequently hear this simple statement while working with people who are in the middle of a difficult conflict or have just come through one. The experience of deep pain, broken relationships, victimization, and violence leave within us a sense of void, anger, and powerlessness.

As in the case of Jacob and Esau (see chap. 1), it may first take years of journeying *away from others* and *within ourselves.* Then we may be able to move toward the source of that pain and toward the people and relationships that created it. Time and timing are intimately connected to reconciliation.

In chapter 4, we heard the voices of Truth, Mercy, Justice, and Peace. Part of their discussion and argument was the question of time, sequence, and proper order. Truth focused on what happened in the past. She understood that for reconciliation we must know and acknowledge the past. Justice argued for action in the present. Both Truth and Justice agreed that they must come before Mercy and Peace.

Peace made the broad affirmation that she was the mother, the spouse, and the child. Mercy claimed that he brought a new beginning. In his view, it was necessary to move beyond the past, embrace a fresh start in the present, and step toward the future. Each had an opinion about how we should understand reconciliation and time as embedded in the past, present, and future of the relationship.

When we approach the question of how time is linked to reconciliation, we are raising complex and intriguing issues. These matters are especially difficult when we are dealing with deep-rooted conflicts bringing violence, victimization, and profound loss. We may be discussing situations of war, crime, or sexual harassment and violation. In such cases, the nature of relationships between individuals and groups has suffered enormous damage.

People experience deep pain, turmoil, and loss. In response, they build layers of protection and insulation. They do this to deal internally with their experience and to defend themselves externally from further anguish and violence. However, the work of reconciliation calls for relationships and a journey through those layers of isolation.

From Concepts to Procedures

How will we rebuild and restore relationships that have been severely damaged through years or even generations of separation and experiences of deep violence? Some people have been actively involved in systematic violence against each other. Their society counted that violence as justified. How do they move toward one another in a new form of coexistence, with mutual respect and cooperation?

In other words, how do enemies reconcile? What kinds of things must happen? When should they happen? In what sequence? Since reconciliation and time are linked, we need to figure out how to make relationships work better, step by step.

Such questions emerge in the context of wars. Hence,

we search for ways to make Truth, Mercy, Justice, and Peace operational. We want them to be more than ideas. We want them to walk on the earth and be visible for entire communities, societies, and nations.

Since the collapse of the Berlin Wall, a symbol that marked entry into a post-Cold War era, the world community has lived through phenomenal changes. In Central America, Eastern Europe, Asia, the Middle East, and Africa, we witness ongoing war and peace. Some countries have made peace accords. In those countries, governments, and the civilian population search for concepts and mechanisms to guide the process of reconstructing the torn social fabric of peoples' lives and communities.

There are few if any effective models of action and frameworks of thinking that emerge from the disciplines of international relations and political or social sciences. Politicians and humanitarians alike turn toward religious, philosophical, and biblically based concepts. They try to make those concepts work at a social and political level.

Thus Sister Peace becomes the National Reconciliation Process. Truth commissions are formed. Brother Mercy takes the form of national amnesty programs. Brother Justice is incarnated in the war tribunals. Each project brings an important aspect of reconciliation. Yet not one of these four colleagues is well understood in practical terms.

I have had opportunities to interact with some of these processes and the people working with them. Without exception, I am challenged and perplexed with the ambiguity and complexity of making operational the journey toward reconciliation in societies torn by war and violence. I find it intriguing that different contexts have connected reconciliation and time in distinct ways. Each culture has its strengths, and each has its challenges.

Let me describe, in broad strokes, three different frameworks of reconciliation. These are not models in the sense that they were explicitly and intentionally designed as reconciliation approaches by the various peoples. Instead, they come from my observations of people dealing with violent situations, as I have interacted with them. Let me tell the story of reconciliation from three different contexts.

1. From Past to Present to Future

In recent years there have been a number of peace processes from which frameworks have been developed. These have some common parallels for moving from deep-rooted violent social and political conflict toward reconstructing the society. The contexts I am referring to include countries like Argentina, El Salvador, and more recently South Africa.

Their commonality lies not so much with the detail or specifics of the respective plans and actions, nor in the similarity of contexts. Each has been quite different. Instead, they share a broad framework of how national and international leaders have thought about what is needed to move from war to peace after enormous violence and injustice. From that thinking, they designed procedures.

My intention in referring to these processes is not to describe in depth or chronologically the events that took place. My interest in the process lies in the exploration of the assumed framework of reconciliation and its understanding about time. I believe reconciliation and time are linked through three elements: The formation of a

Truth Commission and the establishment of *amnesty programs* are undertaken in the framework of a *negotiated peace*.

Peace, in terms discussed in chapter 4, is certainly the mother and the child.

As mother, Peace is recognized as whatever helps establish conditions for negotiation on political, economic, and military issues that have divided the society. At this first level, Peace is equated with a shift in relationship. People stop communicating through guns and start communicating through the spoken word. They declare cease-fires and open negotiations. The parties acknowledge each other and begin to hear out the other's perspectives. They provide space to work through differences in socio-political ways rather than military ways.

As child, Peace is seen as the result, the unfolding process that is given birth by the negotiations. Then in the context of the negotiated peace framework, Truth and Mercy enter the stage.

Truth takes the form of a national commission. In some settings, the commission is formed by people from within the country. In others, it is formed by international participants. Their primary task is to investigate what has happened, particularly in terms of war crimes and abuse of human rights. They are not responsible for providing justice, rectifying matters, or rendering judgment and sentence. Yet civilians who have suffered wrongs and abuses often expect just that.

A Truth Commission is responsible to create space for public and social acknowledgment of the wrongs. In this conceptual framework, people assume that wrongdoing, crimes, and abuse have taken place. The commission recognizes that the society has suffered those abuses, and particularly the victims. They will not be able to heal and move forward without clear, direct, and public recognition of the injustice that has been done.

The society must step from knowing to admitting. The public and social acknowledgment names the evil, identifies the sin, and lists the facts and the perpetrators. All that is deemed critical and necessary for the broader society. In other words, public Truth-telling is needed in the society.

This process differs from spiritually motivated confession in several ways. Spiritual confession is expected to come from the individual's own motivation and is directed toward the person or group offended. In an interpersonal setting, each offender confesses to the offended person or group. Confessions emerge as perpetrators recognize that they did wrong. Such self-awareness creates a desire, conviction, and attitude of repentance. Confession is the mechanism by which the perpetrator makes known personal remorse and regret (Muller-Fahrenholz).

Accountable confession is a third distinct approach. In this case, a Truth Commission is formed by objective outsiders who investigate the events and speak on behalf of Truth in a broad public forum. The motivation to confess does not arise from within the offender. Instead, that individual is investigated in public. The outcome is more like a trial than a process of personal and social transformation. The commission names and speaks the Truth with or (usually) without the perpetrator's internal attitude and remedial action of repentance.

What interests me is the assumed understanding of time and sequencing in all of these approaches to reconciliation. In essence, the Truth Commission is oriented toward the past. Its objective is to establish what happened, who did it, and who was affected. The energy flows toward public recognition and acknowledgment.

In this framework, social reconciliation depends on first establishing and acknowledging the wrong, the wrongdoer, and those who suffered. This procedure is done before moving toward reestablishing relationships and healing. In other words, as spelled out in a New Testament model, confession and acknowledgment precede restoration of the relationship. Healing the social fabric of society begins with public acknowledgment of the wrongs of the past.

Mercy then takes the form of political amnesty and impunity. This is worked out in different ways. In some instances, such as in South Africa, amnesty is offered beforehand as an incentive to encourage individuals to come forward. It is rooted in a message of grace: "If you are truthful and tell us what you and others did, you will not be prosecuted or punished."

In other national processes, amnesty is given consideration only after due process, even forcefully conducted. For example, in Argentina amnesty without punishment was negotiated as part of the peace framework before the Truth Commission took up its mandate. People were guaranteed amnesty as an incentive to speak the truth about what they did, knowing that they would not be punished as a result.

The purpose of amnesty, and the energy and focus of Mercy, is to move beyond the cycle of hatred, recrimination, and vengeance. Peace is fragile. The past must be acknowledged, but present life demands that we start anew. Whatever the operating style, amnesty programs within a framework of a negotiated peace settlement are aimed at giving individuals, groups, and society a new start. Amnesty at least has the practical function of avoiding renewed violence. The principal objective focuses on the present: providing a new start is the minimal goal, and healing is the ultimate goal.

One of the most complicated aspects is the issue of accountability, the voice of Brother Justice. Note that Truth Commissions make public their findings of what happened. However, they do not necessarily decide what should be done with the findings or with the wrongdoers and their leaders. In recent years, war crimes tribunals have emerged to engage in this precise task.

In the case of Bosnia or Rwanda, and as proposed by some for Cambodia and Somalia, people want to establish both public acknowledgment of Truth and accountability on the part of the individuals responsible. This is a complex task, both in terms of technical logistics and ethical dimensions.

Think of the difficult questions it raises. Logistically, one must determine who did what and verify what was done. How will the wrongdoers be found and brought to a court? Under whose jurisdiction do they receive due process?

At the ethical level, other questions are raised. In a context of systematically justified and state-sanctioned violence, how and where do we draw lines of acceptable behavior? There has been massive violence. Will those prosecuted be seen as individuals who acted unethically? Will they be seen as representative scapegoats of targeted groups now under judgment by their enemies or by the international community? Will the process and findings heal the hatreds between peoples and religious bodies? Will they stir up hate and plant seeds for future and more bitter animosities?

As mentioned above, these peace processes have relied on implicit understandings of sequencing and time. In essence, the steps require Peace as the end of fighting, Truth as rendering a public acknowledgment, and Mercy as permitting people of all sides to move back into civil society. That in turn helps to create a deeper and fuller future relationships and reconciliation.

For the most part, Justice as accountability is left out of the operational picture. This often leaves a bitter taste in the mouths of those who were victimized. Then there are worst-case endings without negotiations, where one side wins and the other loses. There "Justice" is often immediate, massive, and generalized, punishing all those connected to the losing side, whether or not they did violent deeds. On the other hand, war crimes tribunals bring extensive documentation and procedures against a reduced number of individuals. Thus at least some persons are held accountable.

In terms of time, this reconciliation framework assumes that we must first establish what happened in the *past,* in order to make it possible to live together in the *present* and move together as a society into the *future.*

2. From Present to Future to Past

Recent history shows that there are no magic wands or formulas that can be applied to the healing and rebuilding of societies moving from war to peace. The past-present-future approach is oriented toward dealing with national issues and the broader civil society that has experienced the war.

This type of reconciling procedure has borrowed parts of a religious and particularly a New Testament style of personal transformation. In practical and expedient ways, it has adapted these elements to working with large groups and societies as a whole.

Nevertheless, the past-present-future model raises a question: How do we get society as a whole to transform and move forward toward sustainable reconciliation? We face the same question on a local level: How do we get people to reconcile if they were former enemies and now live in the same communities? Set aside the big picture of the whole nation. What about our local neighborhood and our local village?

One of the most extraordinary examples comes from the work and efforts of Zoilamerica Narvaez, Alejandro Bendaña, and the Network for Peace and Development in Nicaragua. This Network emerged in the postwar period. Members are demobilized soldiers and their families from both sides of the war. During the conflict, members of the Network fought for the Sandinista government or the Nicaraguan Resistance. They were bitter enemies. Some of them were even assigned to track down and eliminate their counterparts.

The members are mostly lower rank or common foot soldiers who have faced considerable hardships with the beginning of "peace." Since the war, Zoilamerica and Alejandro have worked with people on both sides. They are convinced that sustainable reconciliation and peace must give voice to and include the common person who was a part of the war machine.

In their minds, it is not just a question of reinserting or reintegrating soldiers back into society, as if they are a physical entity being recycled. It is about personal and social transformation that must emerge from within. This involves a process of working with and empowering fighters and their families as actors in creating their own story and place in society. That is better than seeing them as objects of a program. Thus these leaders have worked with the demobilized population to plan and create programs oriented toward their fundamental needs and hopes.

What they found was enormous commonality among the former enemies. The common people on both sides felt left on the margin of society, almost like pariahs. They were encouraged to join the war, and then later they were told to go home and be quiet. They were bitter that national programs rarely responded to the needs of their local communities.

Faced with enormous economic hardship in the country, people watched as one by one their friends returned to the gun, trying to obtain justice through violence. It was the only thing they knew from years of war. The village people shared a suspicion of politicians. They saw their small rural communities collapsing. Day in and day out, they faced basic survival. They felt cast aside. They suffered economic hardship and faced conflict in their local communities. These shared experiences provided common ground for erstwhile enemies to come together.

The Network formed around the two themes that most concerned the former fighters in their communities: How should they deal with conflicts that perpetuate violence and hamper their ability to move forward? How should they create practical solutions to their economic hardship and basic survival needs?

Their answer was to recognize their common plight, work together, and prepare themselves. Over several years, they have formed a national network of local chapters. These chapter leaders are people from both sides of the war. They have received training to be reconcilers and mediators in their own communities.

Former enemies are on local mediating teams to deal with violent conflicts in their villages and districts. They have also received training in developing small enterprises. They elected some of their own members to help administer a fund providing small loans for projects in the villages.

During a training session with members of the Network, I looked into the faces of nearly a hundred people. A few years earlier, they would have been sworn enemies, engaged in a bitter conflict with each other. Five years back, they would have carried guns. Now they were studying how to build peace and create economic development. *How,* I kept wondering, *is it possible for these people to be in this room and work together?* Zoilamerica and Alejandro know the answer. Initially the people were mostly driven by their immediate survival needs.

In this framework for reconciliation, the sequencing of time is understood differently. The common need for survival has created interdependence in the present. The people focus on the present and on what is needed to move toward the future for their families. However, they have almost completely bracketed the past and set it aside for now. It is too close, too painful, and too full of unanswered questions and ambiguous actions.

When the past has come up for consideration, it has caused fights, pain, and disruption. To look at the past only makes the present all the more difficult. They have found, however, that they can develop a relationship based on their common immediate needs. The present provides the possibility of a new relationship and a new beginning.

The present has elements of Mercy, insofar as mercy is understood to mean trying to relate to each other without demanding a recognition of who was right or wrong in the former conflict. Justice has seemed to take two forms. They work together to be accountable to each other now, rather than establishing who should have been held accountable from the past.

This perspective has seemed to emerge in part from an unspoken understanding that they all had good and bad secrets. They have come together to hold their current leaders and politicians accountable for the injustices they feel the rest of society has imposed upon them. Peace has become a primary goal, and they see themselves as direct participants and creators of peace. They have a place and role to play in rebuilding a peaceful Nicaragua.

In the process, Sister Truth has lost her voice. The Network rarely acknowledged or dealt with the past. The past has been put on hold, pushed to the recesses of their minds and experience.

I recall a conversation I overheard at the end of a training session. One participant approached Zoilamerica and asked for a small loan of about ten dollars. "My sister has problems," he said. "At night she cannot sleep. She wanders around and screams in an awful voice that sounds like a monkey. She says there's a monkey inside. She tears at her stomach as if she's trying to get it out. We have gone to medical doctors, but they say there is nothing they can do to get the monkey out. We have heard there is a *brujo* [witch doctor] who can get the monkey out. We need the money to pay him. It's all we know to do."

This story has made a powerful impact on me. It is a metaphor for the depth of pain and suffering caused by violence and war. For these friends in Nicaragua, the past and the war tear at their insides like that monkey. Truth and acknowledgment want out, but it is too painful.

I expect that at some point they will turn and journey back to process that horrible experience. For now, reconciliation, the coming together of former enemies, has focused first on their common needs in *the present*. That has permitted them to move toward and into *the emerging future*. Perhaps at a much later point, they will return to *the past*. As they say, maybe time heals.

3. From Future to Present to Past

In 1994, I was part of a training team that worked with Cambodian officials from all the factions that formed the government then. Most people who participated had directly experienced some aspect of the genocide.

Many saw themselves as victims in one form or another. Many had lost family members. Some carried secrets of their own participation in killing during the great upheaval. Some saw in others their enemies and former oppressors.

During that week, I talked with people individually. I was always curious about their life histories and journeys. Some were willing to share in detail how they survived the violence and low points. Repeatedly, I was amazed at both the similarity of the stories and the incredible endurance of people facing what seemed to be overwhelming odds. This made their current effort more remarkable; they were participating with people whom they had feared and fought against, people who made them suffer.

At the end of each conversation, I raised a question that intrigued me all week. "How can you now work with people who were your enemies?" Often I heard the same answer: "I do it so my children and grandchildren will never have to suffer as we did."

With a focus on future generations, they were able to work with former enemies in the present. However, as each one stated, it was extremely difficult, if not impossible, to talk openly in the meeting about the past in the presence of former enemies. It was far too painful and filled with bitterness. As one person said, "We must keep our eyes on the children."

I was struck then and since with how this implicit approach to reconciliation was distinct and different. The framework of past-present-future suggested that we must first cast out the demon of the past to make peace with our enemies in the present. Yet in Cambodia, the future, the shared common hope for future generations, provided a space within which they could relate and work together in the present. The past, however, was perhaps bracketed even more severely than in the case of the former fighters in Nicaragua.

This has been a common approach in the field of conflict transformation. Talking about the future and what each side needs or desires often provides a greater sense of commonality and less antagonism than talking about the past and who was right or wrong. Reflecting on the future helps create and cultivate the possibility of constructive interaction. Focus on the past often creates reactive and defensive responses. In this style the process of reconciliation moves back from the future through the present to the past.

Visiting our four friends again, we see that Truth, Mercy, Justice, and Peace have been joined by another colleague, Hope. A similar phenomenon occurs in other situations, when people have been victimized through repression and violence as in war, or through deep psychological violence as in sexual harassment. Consistently, their deepest concern seems to be oriented toward two things.

First, they need acknowledgment of the wrong done to them. Second, they are driven by the desire that it never happen to anyone else. It is this intense weight of responsibility for preventing future victimization that motivates a person to engage in the vulnerable journey of confronting the injustice and the enemy. Otherwise, they would prefer to move away from the suffering and forget it.

Within this conceptual framework, Hope sustains and motivates people to take up the challenge of reconciliation in the present. Consider the cases of the Cambodian group and the Nicaraguan friends. Their journey toward the past was for them unbearable if they were to live and work in the present with the very people who represent the image and source of their deepest personal trauma.

However, they are able to focus on hope for *the future* in behalf of others. They want to keep others from experiencing the trauma of their past. This procedure has helped them cope with *the present*. Later, perhaps, they can address *the personally painful past*.

Conclusion

We have looked at three ways that reconciliation and time are linked in the practical experiences of societies and people trying to move from war to peace. Each approach brings insight and a needed perspective to our understanding. Yet within each way are questions, ambiguity, and gaps. Increasingly, I have concluded that we should not rely on a single, rigidly defined operating style. These experiences show that we need a wholistic understanding of reconciliation and time.

A wholistic approach begins with a special set of lenses for looking at time and reconciliation. Those lenses permit us to understand situations with a higher level of complexity and interdependence, grasping several perspectives at the same time. In healing relationships, we have tended to look only for causal formulas based on past-present-future. But reconciliation is not like baking a cake or creating a desired chemical reaction.

This brief exploration, based on listening to the stories and voices of experiences, shows that we need a change of lenses. I have a few tentative prescriptions for those lenses, though I confess that much remains unclear, poorly articulated, and nearly invisible. The departing point, I believe, is to develop a *polychronic* rather than a *monochronic* approach to time, sequencing, and reconciliation.

Anthropologist Edward Hall used the terms *polychronic* and *monochronic* to describe how diverse cultural settings approach and understand time differently (Hall). A monochronic culture has a tendency to do "one thing at a time." On the other hand, people in a polychronic framework work on "multiple things at a time."

The key to polychronic approaches comes in two elements: *multiplicity* of activities and *simultaneity* of action, doing several things at the same time. We need to develop lenses that permit us to see reconciliation and time from a polychronic frame of reference. This requires a *systemic* rather than a *linear* perspective on people, relationships, activities, and context.

With a systemic view, we see people and relationships within a context, a social fabric that is dynamic, interdependent, and evolving. We do not place primary focus on pinpointing the cause, as if that sets in motion a linear reaction. We try to understand the overall system and how change in any one aspect will change all the others. In other words, we have a polychronic, systemic view of reconciliation.

Like a dance, we simultaneously have activities taking place related to the past (Truth), the present (Justice and Mercy), and the future (Hope and Peace). Each contributes and each can change the view of the others and the impact of the others. Each needs a voice. Each depends on the others to reach full potential.

A polychronic approach to time and reconciliation calls for a view of Truth, Justice, Mercy, Peace, and Hope as personal and social *energies*. We have tended to understand these phenomena as principles or values, as if they were static and abstract. Instead, we need to recognize them as continual sources of power and activity that impact individuals and relationships.

Perhaps we are hampered in that we grammatically take them as nouns and objects rather than as verbs. We seek Truth. We do Justice. We extend Mercy. Accordingly, we have the image that each of these is like a material entity. But each actually represents a dynamic process. Considering these concepts as *persons* helps to create an image of live energy, an energy that has a voice and the capacity to act.

For example, instead of Truth being represented by something like one huge rock, Truth-as-person is someone we can walk, talk, and interact with, one we confront, and one who confronts us. Truth is recognized as dynamic energy and becomes just that.

Furthermore, we can begin to imagine these energies as forming an interdependent community. A polychronic view of reconciliation suggests the metaphor of theater and stage. We create a place where the energies of Truth, Justice, Mercy, Peace, and Hope are given life and interact. We need this kind of image to help us see interconnectedness, simultaneity, and interaction as necessary in a polychronic understanding of reconciliation and time.

The image of theater and live voices provides a way to visualize a polychronic understanding of reconciliation. At the end of chapter 4, I described the four persons touching hands and dancing as if around a Maypole. We have this visual image from the stage. The four energies are connected and interdependent.

They are present in the same social space and time. However, they are moving around the central space that connects them, as if circling a pole, a magnet holding them together. In so doing, only one of them at a time comes forward into full view on front stage. Meanwhile, others move backward or prepare to come forward.

With such an image in mind, we can focus our attention on one voice, knowing that to do so does not mean the others are not present or are lost. This is the challenge of polychronicity. We try to create a process and social space that lets us interact with each of the voices while at the same time we stay in touch with all the others.

6
FACING THE POWERS

Do Justice, love Mercy,
and walk humbly with your God.

Not long ago, my home congregation planned to study
the theme of Shalom (peace) at a personal, interpersonal, church, and international level for four Sundays. The
worship committee asked me to bring the Sunday morning message on "Shalom and the Powers."

I balked. "I have a heavy travel schedule and will not
have much time to prepare."

"No problem," they responded. "Just get up and tell
stories. That's all we want to hear anyway."

In a later conversation, I tried to avoid the assignment
and finagle my way around the planners. "I will just have
returned from Latin America, and we have four people
coming in from Colombia, Kenya, and South Africa for
a week of meetings. I won't have time."

"No problem," they repeated. "Just get up and tell stories."

I was reluctant because I always find this topic "Shalom and the Powers" complicated to deal with and understand. It is an area of my work that is ambiguous at
best. I work with powerful people who represent governments. Sometimes I find surprising and engaging relationships. Sometimes I have to deal with manipulation
and evil. I almost always experience tension.

I work with people who are decision makers and power brokers in the very situations I hope to change. How do I respond adequately from my faith values? How do I develop relationships and not compromise those values? I knew, deep down inside, that I did not have any answers to those questions. I almost preferred not to think about that area in too much detail because it might highlight my shortcomings and hypocrisies.

Nonetheless, I recognized this as a good opportunity for me to share my struggle with my own congregation. It was the right thing for me to do. Since I had two months before that Sunday morning, I decided to reread two books. One was Micah, in the Old Testament, which I read almost every day for six weeks. The other was David Chandler's biography of Pol Pot, *Brother Number One* (Chandler).

I decided to follow the advice of the committee. I would simply tell three stories from my own experiences: anecdotes from my interactions with warlords in Somalia, reflections on a recent trip to Cambodia, and dilemmas I faced in working with the U.S. Institute of Peace.

Meeting the Warlords

In the early 1990s, I made numerous trips to Somalia and Somaliland. The area had experienced years of devastating war and was descending into chaos. One of my first trips was soon after the fall of the former dictator, Syaad Barre. I went into Mogadishu during a lull in the fighting, when the United Nations (UN) and most of the international community had left the country.

By this time Somalia had no government and was faced with massive famine caused by the war. I was the guest of a Somalian friend from a minor subclan not aligned with any side of the clan-based factional fighting in the capital at that time. We were traveling on behalf of a committee of Somalians known as the Ergada, with which I had been working for several years. The Ergada had a number of ideas about how to make peace in their country.

During that trip I met with three men. Ali Mahdi claimed to be president, Omar Arti claimed to be prime minister, and General Mohamed Aideed, who had driven the dictator from Mogadishu, insisted that he himself should be president.

As a guest in a Muslim country, I was treated superbly, even in the worst of collapsing conditions. The subclan that had responsibility for me was so careful about my protection and well-being that at times I felt uncomfortable. Everywhere we traveled, two sixteen-year-old boys protected me. One carried a grenade launcher made in the Soviet Union. The other carried a machine gun produced in the United States. As we grew to be friends, I discovered that neither had been in school for the past ten years and neither could read or write. With weapons from East and West, they were a living legacy of the superpowers' Cold War.

I carry several images from those meetings. I have vivid memories of each person taking time to go back over the history of the Somalian conflict. Each then concluded with fiery statements of accusation and justification. Each had been wronged, and each had rights. All of them spoke for the Somalian people.

As I listened, I tried to pick up grains of hope that would show how this war could be ended, how the people could be relieved of suffering. But the people's suffering was always a stepping-stone, a building block for saying, "It's the fault of the other. This is why I must be taken seriously as the true leader."

I shared with one of them my experience of being protected by two sixteen-year-olds. I asked what could be done for the future of the Somalian children. His response was straightforward: "If you and others in the international community will only recognize our government and help us stop our fanatic enemy, we can assure the future of the children."

I asked myself some questions. How can these men justify their actions, when some of their deeds have directly contributed to such massive suffering? Outside the walls where we sat, nearly three hundred thousand Somalians were at risk of starvation. Inside the walls, the leaders debated over who was going to be president. *What of God can I see in these men?* I thought. *What of God can I find here?*

That experience and others led me to a deeper conviction. In Somalia, one could not effectively approach the building of peace by relying exclusively on high-level negotiations between faction leaders. Over the next years, I worked with Bonnie Bergey from Mennonite Central Committee, the Life and Peace Institute from Sweden, and dedicated Somalians inside and outside the country (Sampson and Lederach). For anyone who would take it seriously, we made the case for building peace from the "bottom up" (Heinrich). At the same time, we tried to maintain dialogue with the warlords, but communication was strained and sometimes personalized.

At the second round of UN-sponsored talks in Addis Ababa, we helped to achieve the participation of women, religious leaders, and Somalian nongovernmental organizations (NGOs). Factional and political leaders were not the only ones present in the deliberations for peace. However, General Aideed named me as a person who should not be permitted on the main floor for those deliberations. Over following months, hints came from different sources that it would not be safe for me to return to Mogadishu.

At this writing some seven years later, the UN has pulled back its peacekeeping effort. Fighting between subclans continues in Mogadishu. By the time this book is published, a victor and president may have emerged. Meanwhile, Somalia is a country faced with monumental challenges, a proud people trying to assert control over forces that led to years of suffering and pain.

I have often wondered whether I made the right decisions in Somalia. Should I have spent more time developing relationships with the competing political leaders? Was it right to try to build a base among the Somalian people, who then could confront the leaders? Have I contributed to peace? Have I only prolonged what might be inevitable—that a victor must emerge from among the warlords?

Cambodia

In 1994 I spent several weeks in Cambodia with a training team sponsored by the U.S. Institute of Peace. We met high-level leaders from the four factions that formed the government. Cambodia was one of the few places where the people I worked with were all government related and of high rank. They housed us in the royal palace, where the seminar took place. I slept in the room where Prince Sihanouk once lived, where Pol Pot had held meetings. These extraordinary experiences left me uneasy and struggling.

Sometimes the self-interest of the government officials was quite evident. Other times, I could see that they were genuinely trying to figure out how to reconstruct a country that had been torn asunder by genocide of untold proportions. I felt some of their struggle. Some people saw each other as enemies, but they focused on making the coalition work.

On one hand, they faced tough issues with each other. On the other, they seemed to avoid deeper challenges, particularly those of corruption, graft, and personal power. Such things seemed historically to permeate Cambodian structures of government.

One brilliant colleague with clear-cut opinions, Steve Pieczenik, was a former assistant secretary of state, an expert crisis negotiator, very opinionated, and someone I consider a friend. We connected well, even though we are different in terms of style and philosophical approaches. We never avoided our differences and likely could not have avoided them. We engaged in running conversations about the nature of good and evil and how one deals with evil in the world. Those exchanges served as a backdrop for my experiences during the stay.

Steve thought that the only way to prevent future genocide is through the use of decisive force.

"How do you prevent genocide?" he asked. He immediately answered his own question: "Capture the key perpetrators. Line them up in a public place. Shoot them." Then he asked how I saw it.

I tried to wax eloquent about nonviolence and about working with people at a broader level so leaders cannot manipulate entire situations and populations. I spoke about seeking that of God even where it appears most remote.

It was one thing to have such a conversation while teaching a class at Eastern Mennonite University. It was quite another to have it in Cambodia while working with government officials, some of whom suffered greatly during the genocide and some of whom were perpetrators of it.

One afternoon we visited the genocide museum in Phnom Penh. I have explored other museums in Europe and Israel that capture the essence of such gruesome human history. However, I had never experienced anything that came close to this. The museum is in the school that was converted to a prison and torture chamber when the Khmer Rouge took the city in 1975 on my birthday, April 17.

After the Khmer Rouge took control, an unprecedented set of events took place. First, the major cities of Cambodia were evacuated, literally emptied. The people not shot on the spot were forced to go to the countryside within days. They became known as "the April 17 people." Money markets and private property were abolished. All schools, universities, and Buddhist monasteries were closed. No publishing was allowed. The postal system was abolished. No personal adornment was permitted. Thousands were killed; thousands more died on the roads.

The museum documents the days and activities inside of Tuol Sleng, the school converted into a prison of interrogation and torture. It is estimated that twenty thousand people died in the prison between 1975 and 1979. Each death was documented with full details, providing gut-wrenching stories. The rooms were left just as they were found in 1979. Visitors can walk into rooms that have been essentially untouched.

We moved from one room to the next. At one point Steve asked me, "And what of God do you find here?"

I was silent and thought, *God must have wept.*

The display of broken clocks stuck in my mind. When Pol Pot and the Khmer Rouge took over, they destroyed clocks and calendars. A new Cambodia, a new creation, needed to start from zero. History and time were shattered. The Pol Pot biography depicts the character of this man, *Brother Number One*, in taking it upon himself to start human history over again. "Cambodia would start from zero in an empty city. . . . One had to be part God to start a nation from nothing" (Chandler).

The experience of those people was overwhelming. Everyone in the workshop had suffered through those events. Some had hidden, some had been tortured, and some had been part of the government apparatus but later left. As I walked to the killing fields where genocide had taken place, my sense of logic and understanding was overwhelmed.

The first night we were in Cambodia, we thought we heard a dog outside our dining room. When we asked, we were told that it was a lizard that barks. It made an eerie sound, similar to but stronger than lizards and iguanas I had heard in Central America. Throughout my stay, at about four in the morning, the lizard visited me outside my window. The sound seemed more like a laugh than a bark, a sad haunting laugh about the past.

I wrote a little poem about my Cambodian trip: "The Lizard." It was the only way I knew to deal with feelings that my usual logic could not handle.

Outside my window
the lizard laughs
through the quiet
Phnom Penh dark
filling my
sleepless
night
with the swirl of
voices lost and buried.

Teaching Peace with the U.S. Government

I went to Cambodia as part of a training team from the U.S. Institute of Peace (USIP). In recent years, they have called on me for more input and help than I would have expected in an earlier period. The Institute of Peace was formed by Congress to pursue nonviolent resolution of international conflict.

One of USIP's early proponents in Congress was Dan Glickman, who had a strong Mennonite constituency in central Kansas. The Mennonites encouraged him and others to provide more government emphasis on peace-building and negotiation. However, by the time USIP made it through Congress, Reagan was president. His administration set a more politically conservative and narrow agenda for the Institute. In the past few years, with changing administrations and shifting world contexts, USIP's approach and outreach has broadened.

The Institute of Peace first asked me to deliver a paper at a conference they supported on religion and pacifism. Another time, their training and education department asked me to help them design and deliver their first international conflict resolution training event.

That event brought together representatives from the

diplomatic corps of different regions, the U.S. State Department, humanitarian NGOs, and military officers. They were working with peacekeeping operations in places like Somalia and Rwanda. Later I was asked to be a part of the Cambodian training team.

For me, these were unusual invitations. They put me in touch with people who work at governmental levels in the State Department and with embassies all over the world. Generally, as part of the USIP team, I am asked to describe a framework for conflict transformation and peacebuilding that has evolved from our on-the-ground work internationally.

This framework goes beyond the traditional ways of thinking about diplomacy. It is oriented toward meeting various needs for building peace at different levels of societies divided by deep-rooted conflict and animosity. I believe this approach reflects Anabaptist values and ways of thinking about reconciliation and peacebuilding.

A few years ago, I agreed to be a lead trainer for their next event. The focus was on human crises in settings of armed conflict and collapsing states. It would call together government officials, conflict resolution experts, humanitarian agencies, and military peacekeeping officials from the UN and the USA.

A short time later, my colleague at USIP called to update me on the plans. Through a series of consultative meetings, the War College in Carlisle (Pa.) offered to host the training event. USIP accepted the offer. As he went over the reasons for making this decision, I felt my heart sinking lower and lower.

I told him that I did not think I would be able to take the lead role if it was at the War College. Something just did not feel right. I could come, I said, to provide some input, but I could not see my way clear to be the designer, lead trainer, and one to implement the program.

We went round and round on philosophical concerns and options. I consulted colleagues in my home congregation and at my university. I kept coming back to the same conclusion, based mostly on an inner feeling. In the end, I worked with them on designing the workshop. However, I had only a peripheral role in the event itself.

Since then, I have had "conflicting thoughts" about this decision (Rom. 2:15). On one hand, I think, *Why not take the lead role and go right into the War College?* I often deal with military people in my work. I know they struggle right along with the rest of us in trying to figure things out. To be honest, I often find that they are more receptive and interested in what I have to say about peacebuilding than those in the diplomatic corps.

At times it seemed illogical and foolish not to take the role and help shape everything that was going to happen that week. Nevertheless, I simply had a feeling that it was not right for me to lead an event held at the War College. Did that make sense? The debate went back and forth in my head.

You can participate but not lead? What kind of position is that? Then I would respond to myself, *But how does it fit my basic values, taking on a leadership role, conducting training at the War College, an institution that I hope my work will eventually help transform and eliminate? Where exactly do I draw the line?*

Sometimes I wondered, *Why did I ever get involved in this in the first place? It is so much easier just to keep clear and stay clean.* I found my involvement with the War College to be embarrassing, difficult, and ambiguous.

Conclusions

All three stories point to an obvious fact: I haven't figured many things out. That Sunday morning I asked my congregation not to imagine that my work is clear and correct because I am doing good things. I struggle all the time with ambiguities posed by my work and its connection to people and institutions built on social, political, and military power.

My struggle is shown in a series of dilemmas. Let me illustrate this by returning to the passage in Micah (6:8). I experience at least three dilemmas in terms of my work for peace as I interact with people of political power and the structures within which they work.

First, I no longer feel comfortable with the easily defined two-kingdom theology with which I grew up in the Mennonite Church. Our church approach has often been passed on to me as a theology of separation. We separate church and state through withdrawal and avoidance. We try to avoid the messiness and complications of working and struggling with economic, social, and political policies and processes. We withdraw. We seem to see this as an uncomplicated, easy process.

However, I find this stance too easy and rarely honest. In hundreds of ways, we do participate in the life of society. It is never possible to fully withdraw, and I do not believe we are called to withdraw.

On the other hand, I feel uneasy with and tainted by the compromises that are so easy when we work with high-level political processes and people. I struggle with authenticity and integrity. There is a certain allure and fulfillment that comes with being recognized by officials. It feels good; at the same time, it feels slippery.

This is the *first* set of dilemmas I face, the practical

ones. Where and how do I draw the line so I can work toward bringing kingdom-of-God values into society and also stay clear about our differences and ultimate purpose? How can I wrestle with the challenges of society, develop relationships with those who work in power, and not take part in activities and values contrary to my understanding of faith?

At a second level, as I deal with power structures and people, I struggle with my inner community of prophets and mediators. The prophet in me cries for justice and truth, and the mediator for empathy, understanding, and mercy. Constantly I feel the tension of this dilemma in concrete terms. I can see the oppression and injustice that people choose to inflict on others. I see the structures within which powerful people move and from which they benefit. Yet all of these people are also children of God, even warlords and dictators with whom I work, whom seem so set in their ways. I seek to understand them, "hoping against hope" (Rom. 4:18) for change and transformation.

This then is a *second* set of dilemmas, as I face the heritage of faith. How can I be true to myself and my faith while maintaining relationships with fellow humans, even enemies, and seeking that of God in each? How do I relate to others as persons within structures of power that I believe should change for the sake of Truth and Justice? To what degree is it possible to work with them and still seek personal and structural transformation? How and when do I know when I have crossed the line and gone beyond the bounds of authenticity?

At a personal level, I struggle with a *third* set of dilemmas regarding opportunities and choices in my work. When is an invitation or piece of work an opportunity to bring the message of reconciliation to people at a high level who need to hear it? When is my ego being fed by recognition, prestige, and power? So often the two are mixed. Is that good or bad, right or wrong?

With these dilemmas and ambiguities on my mind, I return to the book of Micah. In my two months of reading Micah, something struck me: five times Micah refers to walking. The first is an admonition to those of faith who have turned from God. Micah proclaims, "You shall not walk haughtily" (2:3).

The second, third, and fourth times mention the search for seeking to walk in God's paths: "For all the peoples walk, each in the name of its god, but we will walk in the name of the Lord our God" (4:5; cf. 2:7; 4:2).

The final reference comes full circle back to the first (2:3). "Do justice, love mercy, and walk humbly with your God" (6:8, NRSV/KJV). Micah believed in the journey, the walk toward and with God.

I have often reflected on this text. Only while thinking about power did the third component appear as the key. I see the idea of "walking humbly" as a key because it helps to situate me, my attitude, and my demeanor. To walk in the paths of God is an evolving journey of faith. I believe this journey takes us into the world, not away from it. In Mennonite circles we often talk about being "in the world, but not of the world" (John 17:6-19). Too often that has meant that we withdraw and remove ourselves from the world. I believe it means something quite different.

To be in the world but not of the world, we must face the challenge of the dilemmas I posed earlier. We cannot respond by withdrawing from the messiness of the world. Instead, we are called to bring God's love into the world. We do this through who we are and how we walk. According to Micah, we are to walk humbly. I understand this in a literal way. While I seek to walk with God, I recognize that I simply do not understand it all. I am not a miracle worker. I do not have crystal-clear vision. I do not have all the answers. I am not God; I am a mortal.

This is the fundamental example of Jesus. Though he was in the form of God, he did not regard equality with God as something to be exploited (Phil. 2:6). Is this not walking humbly, that we do nothing from selfish ambition, but regard others along our path as better than ourselves?

While working with people of power, I have witnessed the process of humans wishing to be God and trying to replace God. That, I think, is the single most significant pitfall of political power. It is frightening to recognize that I am a lot like them. I confess that the real struggle is not so much doing justice or loving mercy, but walking humbly in this world, as a fellow human and child of God.

I am not sure I have made the right decisions in Somalia, Cambodia, or other places I have worked. The situations and relationships I have tried to deal with can be understood in more than one way. I have come to appreciate such ambiguity. It is good for one's soul. Ambiguity means that I am not always clear about how I should respond to opportunities for working at reconciliation, particularly those that involve people in positions of power.

To journey toward reconciliation, we must enter the stream of their lives and walk with people who created conflict and are affected by the conflict. We live in a messy and violent world that needs the presence of something different. I hope my feet have stayed on the holy path that God walks, though I know that at times they have wandered about in the messiness, trying to find the path.

Holiness, unlike ambiguity, calls for distinction, clarity, and choices. Holiness is tough work, but it is also good for one's soul. I think the central dilemma we face in the church is the tension between ambiguity and holiness. Too quickly we assume that these are incompatible choices. I have chosen to keep ambiguity and holiness together, rather than choosing one over the other.

The only way that is feasible is to follow the words of Micah: Keep up the journey, but walk humbly, for we are walking as one among many. And we are walking with God.

PART 2

THE
JOURNEY
THROUGH
CONFLICT

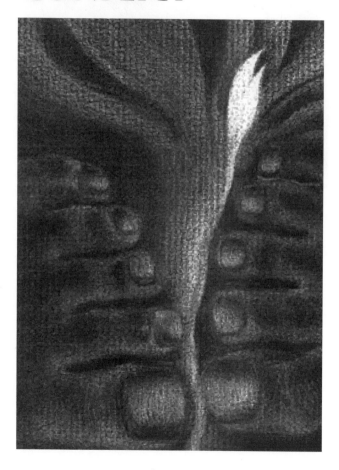

7

CONFLICT IN THE CHURCH?

$everal years ago, I worked with a congregation that was experiencing a crisis over worship and pastoral leadership. Two opposing groups had formed. Some people were struggling to avoid joining one or the other.

Some people felt strongly that the pastor's leadership was inadequate, in large part because he came from "an old style" and was not open to more expressive forms of worship. They felt left out, "unfed." To them, every Sunday service felt like the same format with little participation or innovation.

"How can the Spirit move and find the freedom to change and motivate us?" they asked. "All we ever sing is four-part harmony. What about some songs with enthusiasm and instruments? Maybe even with a beat?" They thought the church needed a change, and that changing the pastor would be a good place to start.

Others felt comfortable with the current leadership and style. They saw the pastor as mature, steady, and providing a sense of security and support.

"We are not interested in some kind of wild Sunday service," they commented. "After all, God is a God of order," one person stated. They appreciated the litanies and hymns. "Off-the-wall singing is off the wall, frivolous." In their view, if the church needed change, the need was for some others to change congregations and quit raising a ruckus.

We agreed to work together for several months in exploring members' basic concerns, fears, and hopes. Early in the process, we held a congregation-wide meeting that lasted most of the afternoon and well into the evening. First we heard the concerns of several people representing different views and concerns. Then we had an extended open period for people to express whatever they needed to say.

I listened carefully and asked people to explain in more detail what they meant or had experienced. When we finished, we had not reached any agreement or consensus, but we had a better understanding of the various viewpoints.

As I was about to leave the building, a young man approached me. He had not spoken during the meeting. In church fights, many people feel it is important to give the outside consultant some special and ever-so-important tidbit of insight. He wanted to help me understand the "real story" of what had been going on. What he said has stuck with me. In many ways, it represents a common view of conflict in the church.

He spoke softly to make sure only my ears heard. "You know, the real problem we have is that some people here are not right with God. If they got right with God," his hand pointed toward the ceiling, "things would clear up here." His hands pointed to the surrounding people and sanctuary.

During years of consulting, I have found this to be a common view of conflict in church circles. Conflict is sin. It shows that people are falling from the straight and narrow way. Working with and through conflict is essentially a matter of making sure people "get right with God."

My experiences have led me to question this rather

spiritualized view and to appreciate a different biblical and theological understanding of conflict. Typically, we have not looked into conflict as a theological issue to be explored. Usually we simply count a party in opposition to "our group" to be also in opposition to God.

Anabaptists have long held a "peace" stance. Our shelves are filled with volumes on the theology of peace, but our history is full of conflict. Conflict extends from the early and violent days of the sixteenth century to our multiple divisions and continuing schisms. In our history, we have a "Sacred Hidden Closet of Church Growth by Splitting."

We have been a rather contentious bunch, but we do not have a clear theology of conflict. Our shelves have few books on conflict. Most people in our circles probably understand conflict and faith like the young man mentioned above.

I am convinced that, when faced with conflict, many of us in the church operate by a series of understood but unexpressed rules and guidelines. Since they emerged in my own denominational experiences, I have called them the "Unspoken Ten Commandments of Conflict in the Mennonite Church." They likely fit many other churches and church organizations, too.

The Unspoken Ten Commandments of Conflict in the Mennonite Church

1. Thou shalt be nice. Always be nice. Yea, I say unto thee, "niceness" is the essence of Christianity.

2. Thou shalt not confront each other in public. Confrontation is nasty and unmanageable. If ever in doubt about confrontation, refer to commandment number 1.

3. Should thou ever have the distasteful experience of confrontation, thou shalt not listen to thine enemy, but shalt prepare thy defense while the enemy is still speaking. Yea, I say unto thee, listening raises questions that weaken thy defense and may lead to compromise, impurity, and, heaven forbid, self-reflection. It is dangerous to change thy mind or admit that thou wert wrong. Truth is unchangeable.

4. Speak not with contentious folks who disagree with thee or who have raised thy "righteous" anger. Thou shalt seek out and talk to others about them. Yea, more, dear brothers and sisters, speak only with nice people who agree with thee. By speaking only with those with whom thou dost agree, thou wilt experience the true support of community.

5. Remember that thou art of noble and decent character, even a pacifist, and thou shalt not show thine emotions in public.

6. Men, be rational. Do not show weakness through emotions like crying or anger. It is better for thee to disengage from a situation of conflict and remain silent than to show uncontrolled emotion.

7. Women, thou shalt not defend thyself vigorously, nor "nag" incessantly, or they may call thee the dreaded *B* word. Thou shalt be prepared to have thine opinions ignored, realizing that those same opinions may be accepted as valid if later stated by a man. Thou shalt not gripe about this in the presence of men.

8. If thou dost not like the way things are going in the church, thou shalt blame the pastor. Most problems can be traced to the pastor. If the pastor is a saint, then blame the church council. If the church council is clean, then blame "them." Keep it a generic and undefined "they" or "some people I know." If thou cannot find anyone to blame, leave the church. Verily, I say, a church where there is nobody to blame is not worth staying in.

9. If thou must confront, save thine energy, frustration, and irritation for the annual budget meeting. God gave annual budget meetings to bring congregational catharsis.

10. Dear Christian sisters and brothers, in a holy nutshell I say unto ye all, thou shalt not have conflict in the church. Conflict is a sign of sin. Yea, should conflict emerge, pray that God may convict and convert thine erring enemies.

This list looks with humor at our behavior, but I believe these Ten Commandments describe many people's experiences. Such patterns may even come too close for comfort. In part, that is because these commandments connect with some typical responses that form the underpinnings, not of what we say we *believe*, but of what we actually *do* with conflict. What we actually do is our practice, or *praxis*.

The core of this praxis returns to the young man's comment. Conflict is painful and messy. We may deal with the uncertainty of messiness on a *theological* level, by suggesting that conflict is primarily a question of sin, "their" sin.

At a *personal* level, we deal with the pain and anxiety by finding a variety of clever ways to avoid facing the conflict. We find justifications for moving *away from* rather than *toward* conflict. Too often we adjust our theology to match what we actually do. To support avoidance, we cite biblical clauses, using them detached from their context: "Have nothing to do with anyone who causes divisions" (Titus 3:10-11).

I understand Anabaptism as a down-to-earth way of looking at things. It is incarnational in nature. We say, "What you do and how you act is a window into what you believe." We stress following Jesus in daily life.

Nevertheless, in the Unspoken Commandments, we face a paradox in our congregations. On one hand, we claim that we want our church community to discern what is God's will. We say that we see, discern, and interpret God's presence and leading in our lives through a communal process. This process connects individual insight, prayer, and the Bible with talking and testing insights through and in community.

On the other hand, our usual practice often suggests that we put a low value on disagreement, diversity, and confrontation until things heat up. Then we put high value on the moral and righteous grounds, since "we are right." Our understanding of the Bible demands transparency, respect, listening, and a high tolerance for uncertainty as fuller insight into Truth emerges. In practice, however, we have rarely developed these as valued skills.

The Unspoken Commandments are not exclusive to church circles. Social scientists claim that they are rooted in a series of common dynamics that accompany conflict as it escalates (Hocker and Wilmot). The fundamental idea is that conflict changes things (Mennonite Conciliation Service). It transforms perceptions, communication, relationships, and the structure and organization of groups. Consider some of the more important changes that conflict can produce.

Change 1
When we are in a healthy relationship, we are able to do several things well as we face differences and disagree-

ments. We can acknowledge openly that a conflict exists. We share responsibility for facing it. We work together on the issues.

However, when the argument heats up or when we feel questioned or threatened, our defenses go up, and a first change sets in. Rather than sharing responsibility for the problems with the other person, we begin to see *the other person as the problem.* We question what he or she is up to. We wonder, sometimes out loud, "What is your problem?" It's no longer just a disagreement. We feel personal antagonism.

This simple change is subtle but lies at the root of how conflict can move in divisive and destructive directions. If we primarily or exclusively (as happens far too often) operate with the idea that the other person is the problem, the solutions are to change the person, to get away from the person, or in the worst scenario, to get rid of the person.

Too often we see conflict as a battle to be won instead of a problem to be addressed in the relationship. We think that if we eliminate the person, we eliminate the problem. This viewpoint starts with the first common shift in the early stage of conflict: seeing the other person as the problem.

Change 2

The second major change is what happens to the issues. Have you noticed what pops into your mind when somebody confronts you? "Yeah, and what makes *you* such a saint? Why, just last week I saw you . . ."

Suddenly you raise a different issue that shifts attention away from the questions your friend has just posed. She may then counter by adding another concern that bothers her. The discussion feels confused and tangled. You both move from one topic to the next, without conclusion or clarity.

Issues multiply. This is common as conflict progresses. We pull in more issues. We can easily feel overwhelmed and unclear about what, exactly, this conflict is about.

One central tension in many conflicts is about *which*, of the many issues, is the *real* problem. This may be why we describe conflict as a "mess" or "a can of worms," where creepy and slimy things just keep crawling out. Many people respond to conflict with simple advice: "Don't open that can. Avoid the messy confusion."

Change 3

A third dynamic is the way our language changes as conflict escalates. Because we see the other person as the threat, we begin to project blame onto "you." Pay attention to how the accusing and even finger-pointing form of "you" increases as people get angrier and more intensely involved in the conflict. "*You* are so irritating." "*You* make me so angry."

I have found this particularly true at home. From time to time I have heated discussions with my wife or children. Yes, we have a good number of verbal fights at home! I have had many years of training, education, and experience in mediation. In spite of that, I so easily fall into a blaming and projecting mode. I know this is happening when I hear *you* in the beginning of my comments: "*You* . . ."

Along with projecting blame, our language tends to become more generalized as conflict escalates. We talk in less-specific terms about the issues and the people. We stereotype by saying "they." We put people in a unit and describe them in broad, general strokes. For example: "Well, you know, that's just how those charismatics are."

It's always easier to maintain a defensive stance about the other side when we operate with stereotypes and generalizations. As issues increase and language gets more general, people are less sure of what is really going on and how to respond. At the same time, they feel increasingly threatened and defensive.

Change 4

A fourth major change begins as we talk with like-minded persons about our problems and conflicts. This is natural to all groups and societies, though it takes different forms. Instead of talking directly with the people with whom we have the problem, we talk to others *about* them.

This is a key shift in communication that soon becomes obvious to those talked about. We thus avoid direct confrontation. In some cultures, open confrontation is seen as distasteful, impolite, and socially irresponsible. One is not supposed to cause another person to lose face. However, if you confront someone else, you must expose that person.

In other settings, *not* confronting is seen as a lack of responsibility. In either case, or for whatever reason, if you don't go to the person directly but speak to others, more people are involved. That makes the situation more complex.

In church settings, this dynamic is in line with several of our Unspoken Commandments. As tensions escalate, we tend to move away from discussion of controversial issues and away from those who do not agree with us. We move toward friends who agree with us. We are nice in public, but we talk behind the backs of others because we do not have the skill or the will to address our differences directly. In other words, we stoop to backbiting (Rom. 1:30; 2 Cor. 12:20; KJV).

Change 5

A fifth dimension changes the nature of our response. We respond to the situation according to the latest "thing" that "the other side" has done. We focus on responding to their latest action or comment. The conflict moves away from originating and core issues. The pattern sets in motion a cycle of action-reaction that operates almost on its own energy.

This can be accompanied by a change in goals, though we rarely discuss our goals openly. In the worst settings, people move from feeling personal antagonism toward more direct forms of hostility. In some cases, these may be open forms of violence. In others, the expressions of hostility may be indirect, as in psychological warfare.

Our initial goal was to understand the issues and each other. Our new goal is to win, get revenge, and do harm to the other. Everyone involved experiences a deep and real sense of threat that produces insecurity and doubts about ourselves.

Change 6

Eventually, conflict can change the social organization of a group. The process of "moving away" is no longer just an individual thing. Often the original group splits into two opposing groups. People feel pressure to be on one side or the other: "You are either with us or against us." Sides form as clear groups emerge. There is almost no middle ground.

Some who are thought of as extremists at an early stage

later become leaders. Communication patterns change. When conflict is fully escalated, people tend to talk only with those who agree with them. They have little contact with differing viewpoints. Consequently, each group is increasingly dependent on indirect information about what others are thinking. There is less accurate communication.

Summary

These sociological patterns create certain common outcomes if they are carried on unabated. As conflict escalates, people tend to distrust and move away from those who are perceived to hold different views or are creating the discomfort. There is less direct and accurate communication.

Conflict is painful and threatening. The worst expressions of hostility can be psychologically damaging and physically violent. In practical terms, these Unspoken Commandments and social patterns show why we carry negative images of conflict. We usually do everything possible to avoid it.

Our patterns and beliefs about conflict pose a number of intriguing questions. Does biblical theology back these unspoken rules and practices? Or is there a biblical vision that questions our practices? Is it possible to understand conflict as a necessary and positive element in our lives? Is conflict a sign of sin that must be cut from our lives?

In the next few chapters, I will explore these questions by looking into conflict through windows opened by biblical stories and teachings. These passages give us an overview of a biblical understanding of conflict.

8

IN THE BEGINNING . . . WAS CONFLICT

In the beginning God created, Genesis tells us. From a formless void, the winds of the Creator gave shape to the earth. God separated light from darkness, marking the start of time and history. He separated land from water. The dome of the sky separated upper and lower waters. Plants, animals, birds, and fish of every kind were brought forth. Then the miracle of human presence emerged; *we* were created in the image of God (Gen. 1:27).

Volumes have been written about this marvelous act of God. I do not propose to undertake a scholarly exegesis of Genesis 1. Yet I am always struck with the centrality of this event as related to how we understand who we are, how we live and interact, and the original intention of God in creating human history. I also believe this creation story has much to do with developing a theology of conflict. Let me make three observations in the form of affirmations about this theology embedded in Genesis 1.

First and most important is the notion that we are created in the image of God. There is "that of God" in each of us. How can we begin to fathom this idea that we, fragile and finite beings, somehow are like the God of history? There are many ways to approach the "image" dilemma. It is instructive to start with the more self-evident question: *What*, literally, is God doing? This is better than trying to answer the far more complex question: *Who* is God? If we see what God is doing, we will have at least some idea of the nature of God in whose image we have been created.

The immediate answer is quite simple. God is creating. This then begs another question: What does it take to create? I believe that the process of creation is built on several different levels of activity and meaning.

Creation starts with an idea. It calls for the capacity to think, reflect, and plan. In other words, this involves projecting an idea beyond oneself. Creation is also connected to feeling. It is not simply an "idea" in the mind. It is a feeling at a deeper gut level. We are "moved" to do something. We feel the idea. In other words, creation is rooted in *passion* and *caring*.

At another level, creation calls for action. "Let's move on that idea," we say, with some passion. Action is movement. It is purposefully carrying forward activity to *realize* the idea. Like the process of birth, it takes something that was envisioned but not physically seen, heard, or felt, and brings it out into the world of sight, sound, and touch. Creation is an act.

When we look at the Genesis story, we see these same basic elements. God envisions and projects, reflects and plans. God feels and cares with passion. And God moves and acts in history. We too have these basic abilities. We are endowed with the capacities of thinking, reflecting, projecting, and acting. We act in history. In fact, we create the very history that we ourselves experience as real. We are ongoing co-creators of our own history, some of it for good and some of it for evil. Nonetheless, we are participants.

In Genesis we find that God makes a series of creation commitments. These are specific characteristics or dynamics in the way God has envisioned and built our world. Here are three *creation commitments* to discuss in more detail:

Commitment 1:
God Present Within Each of Us

In the most significant act of creation, we were created in the image of God. In this act, we find the fundamental commitment that there will be that of God in each of us. We see this through the characteristics present within us that reflect the Creator: We are each provided with the capacity to think, reflect, feel, care, and act.

We can, in a most profound way, affirm what Jacob says in his encounter with his brother: "To see your face is to see the face of God." Humanity and each of us as persons are given the gift of life, a gift that carries within it and within us the presence and touch of God. There is that of God within each of us. As early Quakers taught, in peacemaking we need to "speak to that of God in every person."

Commitment 2:
God Valuing Diversity

The second affirmation lies in the profound understatement that God created us "male and female." "Aha!" some will say. "Now we see the connection between Genesis 1 and conflict." There is a useful and important body of literature and research on gender differences and conflict. However, I am more interested here in the basic truth present in the creation story, that God brought forth diversity.

Differences and distinctions permeate the creation account. In the first chapter of Genesis, the phrase "of every kind" appears ten times, referring to seeds, plants, birds, fish, and animals. I am left with the overall picture of a rain forest, full of almost infinite varieties of life, or of a coral reef teeming with diverse creatures.

At another level are the careful distinctions to provide order and meaning. Light brings day and night. Earth is separated from the sky. The sky separates upper and lower waters. Water and land are moved apart. Each element is distinct from the other and yet only has identity and meaning as connected to each other in relationship.

The culmination of this process is the creation of humankind as male and female. This simple beginning becomes one of God's firm and consistent commitments. If you look around your family and blood relatives, those closest to you, you cannot find another person that is exactly like you. If you search your community and even your nation, still you will be unique. Six billion people inhabit Earth (by June 16, 1999), and yet not one is exactly like the other.

You can turn your sights back across history to the beginning of time, only to realize that there has never been one person created and living completely like another. Fraternal twins, for all their similarities, have distinctions and unique features. Identical twins are soon shaped by varied experiences. God has valued and continues to value diversity.

Commitment 3:
God Giving Us Godlike Freedom
The third affirmation is found in the tree of the knowledge of good and evil (Gen. 2:9, 17). This tree is often seen as the precursor to the Fall and the entry of sin into the garden of Eden (Gen. 3). Humans were not satisfied

with what God had given them and sought to be "like God" (Gen. 3:5). We usually jump to the consequences of Adam and Eve's decisions. If we do so, we overlook the profound insight that God, in creating them, was committed to providing them with freedom of choice.

Perhaps more than any other characteristic, this commitment defines the very nature of God and the image in which we have been created. God is free, free to do and to choose and to act. In this sense, the tree was necessary in order to provide the choice. This is the reality of freedom. Without opportunity, without choice, without freedom, humankind loses its unique place in the creation. We are created in the image of God to the degree that God was committed to giving us a Godlike freedom.

Humankind a Dynamic Mix

On the surface, each of these creation commitments seems self-evident and rather simple. Combined, however, they make for quite a mix. Each human was created in the image of God with the capacity to think, reflect, project, feel, and act. And yet each was created as a unique individual, and each had the freedom to choose. All of this was built into the creation before the Fall.

Let us take a step back for a moment and consider the significance of this aspect of creation. With purpose and for fun, I have approached this issue in seminar formats with two illustrations, each involving a question.

First I ask the audience to compare a colony of ants and a colony of Mennonites or of the listeners' own church. I want them to identify what distinguishes humans from animals. At first, with laughter, they respond with similarities. "We work hard. We live in communities. We know how to farm. We are pragmatic and want to get things done. We all look alike."

Next come the distinctions. "We think and feel, but ants act by instinct. We have choices and dreams. We are quite diverse within our own species. Each of us is a person, unique, with a soul and a mind and a Godlikeness." We note how much more dynamic and rich our life and experience is than that of ants, because we have this Godlikeness, and we are individuals with minds, hearts, and souls.

Then I add, "Oh, by the way, within their colony, ants don't fight." A number of times entomologists at some length have clarified the scientific facts around such a sweeping comment. With good humor, we usually agree that ants do not experience conflict like humans do.

Then as a second step, I ask them to use a process of imagination. "Imagine for a moment," I say, "that you have been asked by the national government to build the perfect factory. You will be given all the natural and human resources you need. There will be no impediment to whatever you wish to try. How would you construct the perfect factory?"

The question is probing the issue of our natural inclinations as we think about building the perfect world. What regularly emerges is our temptation to put robot workers in the ideal factory. The place would work mechanically and without a hitch. People would be asked to do a particular job, but not to think, dream, or make many choices. All the choices are already made. People are asked to follow instructions and make the product.

How interesting and ironic that such a place is set up to eliminate diversity and choice! It also eliminates conflict. Read major novels about the future, like *1984* or

Brave New World. See how the authors conceive of paradise as a place where conflict does not exist. To achieve such a condition in these worlds, the author wipes out diversity and individuality, to restrict imagination and choice. In other words, it is the *exact opposite* of God's creation commitments: Godlikeness in each, unique diversity for all, and freedom throughout.

On the sixth day, God looked over this creation and said, "It is very good." Quite frankly, it was a mess, a dynamic, rich, and wonderful mess. In my view, this is the central point of the creation commitments. The very elements that make human experience rich and dynamic, the characteristics missing in the experience of ants, are the elements that make conflict inevitable. Conflict is natural.

I believe this is the key to a "Genesis window" for viewing conflict. By the very way we are created, conflict will be a part of our ongoing human experience.

Let us push this a bit further. Most of us recognize that conflict is a part of our lives and relationships today. However, there tends to be a common and rather strong perspective within Christian circles that conflict is sin. Recognition of our fallen nature leads to the general perspective that conflict is sin. On the other hand, the Genesis window and God's creation commitments provide a different viewpoint. Built into God's original plan *before* the Fall, humankind was conceived in such a way that made differences and conflict inevitable.

Adam and Eve were naming the animals and plants, feeding themselves, filling the earth, and being fruitful and multiplying. Can you imagine that they went about their tasks without disagreement and argument? Both were created in the image of God. Each was an individ-

ual, and each had freedom. Can you really imagine that
they never argued or disagreed? How utterly boring, if
that were the case!

The Genesis story sets the stage for conflict as a natural part of our relationships because of who we are, as
God created us. Conflict in itself is not sin. But sin may
enter into the situation, depending on how we approach conflict, how we deal with it, and especially how
we treat each other.

The signs of sin entering conflict appear when we act
like God or want to be God, when we assume superiority, when we oppress, when we try to lord it over others,
when we refuse to listen, when we discount and exclude
others, when we hold back deep feelings, when we
avoid, when we hate, and/or when we project blame
with no self-reflection.

In sum, the Genesis window on conflict is built on
these basic creation commitments: God is present in
each of us. We are created in the likeness God. God values diversity. God is committed to give us freedom.
These elements make our lives rich, ever-renewing, and
interesting. They also make conflict a natural part of our
relationships.

9

WHERE TWO OR THREE MEET

I grew up in Hubbard, Oregon. As a child, I thought that was like living in paradise. Most Oregonians feel this way, and so apparently did many Californians who moved north to Oregon. But that is a conflict we will not explore here. I was a Mennonite PK, a preacher's kid.

In rural Oregon, being a PK meant considerable participation in church activities. That created points of contention for an eight-year-old: No watching *Wonderful World of Disney* on Sunday evening. No playing baseball during summer Bible school week in June. Always attending Wednesday evening prayer meeting, even though few others came.

In the Sunday and Wednesday evening services, I first heard, enough times to memorize it, the well-known verse from Matthew 18:20: "For where two or three are gathered in my name, I am there among them." Years later, I again heard these verses used on "the mission field," by small, fledgling congregations in different parts of the globe. I think it is the most-quoted verse from Matthew 18.

It is used in a fairly consistent way across cultural and geographic contexts, to encourage a small gathering for worship. They take it to mean, "Hey, it doesn't matter if only a few of us have shown up. Take courage. God is among us."

It is true that we do not need large numbers of people

for God to be present. God is present with me even when I am completely alone. But what is the meaning of these verses in the context of Matthew 18? When this verse is understood in the flow of the whole passage, its meaning is quite different from its typical use for encouragement because few people are present. The context is *conflict*.

Matthew 18 is a chapter about conflicts. Consider for a moment the stories and teachings. The chapter begins with the disciples asking the question, "Who is the greatest in the kingdom of heaven?" They are primarily concerned with status and power. Who will stand higher than another? Who will be seen as more important? Think for a minute about your own experiences with organizations, church structures, governments, and the like. Conflicts over power and status occur all the time.

At the end of the chapter, Jesus relates the parable of the unforgiving servant. Here is a man who owes a large sum of money to the king. The debtor begs for mercy and patience. The king, we are told, has pity and has forgiven him his entire debt. Minutes later, this same man bumps into a neighbor who owes him a small sum of money. He leaps at his throat and demands to be paid right away. His friend begs for mercy, but to no avail. The king, upon hearing this, throws the man in prison for his lack of mercy.

The conflict is over money and payment schedules. Does this sound much like conflicts in the church over money, debts, and payment schedules? Matthew 18 starts with power and ends with money. The entire chapter deals with mundane, human, relational dynamics that lie at the root of most conflicts. In the middle of chapter 18, we find verses 15-20:

If another member of the church sins against you, go and point out the fault when the two of you are alone. If the member listens to you, you have regained that one. But if you are not listened to, take one or two others along with you, so that every word may be confirmed by the evidence of two or three witnesses. If the member refuses to listen to them, tell it to the church; and if the offender refuses to listen even to the church, let such a one be to you as a Gentile and a tax collector. Truly I tell you, whatever you bind on earth will be bound in heaven, and whatever you loose on earth will be loosed in heaven. Again, truly I tell you, if two of you agree on earth about anything you ask, it will be done for you by my Father in heaven. For where two or three are gathered in my name, I am there among them.

Practical Guidelines

These interesting verses give direct and practical teaching from Jesus. They provide specific guidelines for how we are to proceed when we feel we have been wronged or when we feel that a sister or brother has erred.

As I ponder these verses, I have certain limitations and advantages that a theologian does not have. By training, I am a sociologist. So I put on lenses that look for the structure and dynamics of social process and the spiritual dimension that underpins these processes. I do not, however, have the tools of rigorous biblical interpretation. So please bear that in mind as I outline my observations.

I take the statement "If another member of the church *sins*" in a broad sense (any sinning) rather than a narrow sense (only if sinning against you). This is justified because "against you" (18:15) is not in the oldest Greek texts, biblical students tell me (see the NRSV note). Peter is the one who seems to be chiefly concerned about someone who sins "against me" (18:21). But I think Jesus had a broad concern for gently restoring *any* transgressing member (as in Matt. 5:23-24; 7:5; Luke 17:3; cf. Gal. 6:1; Lev. 19:17; Ezek. 3:16-21).

Anyhow, in most conflicts and especially in those involving church members, almost everybody on all sides of the problem feels that they have been sinned against. I have found this to be true, especially if the conflict has gained any momentum or has escalated.

Here in Matthew 18, a church member wants to bring correction to another member regarded to have done something wrong. I understand "sins (against)" to imply that we have a conflict in the making. I want to look into these verses for what light they shed on how we understand and respond to conflict.

As a sociologist who works from a faith basis, I have several questions. Exactly how do these steps guide us in thinking about and approaching conflict? What assumptions underlie the steps? What goals are to be achieved? What dynamics do they clarify about relationships and handling confrontation?

What skills does Jesus assume we need? What challenges does this approach pose for us? Is this model good for all situations and cultures? How does our actual behavior look alongside the suggested guidelines? What, in the end, is the window of wisdom and light that this instruction opens on conflict? Let me start by making four basic observations.

First, in the context of the chapter and this particular teaching, the primary and ultimate goal of this teaching is to work for reconciliation. We are called to work for the restoration and healing of people and their relationships.

Second, in my opinion, these are some of the most specific and practical guidelines appearing in all the teachings of Jesus. He is not talking in parables or providing broad principles. He has identified four specific steps in a detailed order.

Third, this is one of the few times that Jesus mentions, in a specific way, the church or the organized community. As such, this text outlines specific steps for how people in the redeemed, peaceful community should handle differences, confrontation, and conflict.

Fourth, while Jesus' instruction here is eminently practical, it is rarely practiced. Indeed, it is one of the least-practiced teachings in the New Testament. Let me illustrate this latter point by providing you with Matthew 18:15-20 in the NPV (Normal Practice Version), written from the pews of the First Mennonite Church of Normal Practice.

> When you have a problem with somebody in the church, check it out first to make sure you are not alone in this problem. There is a good chance that if you have had a problem with this person, somebody else has as well. Go and pick a good friend who is likely to understand and agree with you. If she agrees with you that this person is a real turkey, then talk to some more people to see if there is broader consensus. If money, land, or inheritance is involved, tell it to a lawyer, as lawyers were given by God to keep the church honest. If a friend, a small group, and a lawyer agree, then tell it to the church, preferably in private to the pastor and elders. When you tell them, say it is a concern that you have prayed about for some time and that there is a group of people who share the concern. Do not tell it openly in a congregational meeting since that is volatile and could get messy. Truly I say to you,

from that point on, it is the responsibility of the pastor and elders to take care of the problem. Your task is to make sure they do it right.

The contrast between the New Revised Standard Version and the Normal Practice Version shows many ways we tend to *avoid* and actually *extend* the conflict within the community. We avoid the specific procedures in Jesus' original teaching that lead to engagement, a turning toward conflict and the other. Let us look at each step and its implications in more detail.

Step 1: Going Directly

This seems to be a logical and straightforward idea. Yet *talking with* the person *about* the problem represents one of the more difficult practical interactions in human relationships. In common practice, complainers take the problem outside the relationship and "triangle" other people into the situation. While it seems simple to go directly and talk with the brother or sister, that is actually based on a number of important prerequisites and assumptions. To understand those requires scrutiny from social, psychological, and spiritual dimensions.

From the social and psychological viewpoint, to engage someone in direct conversation about a problem I have with him or her requires a double movement. First, I must begin an internal process of awareness, dealing with my own feelings, anxieties, and perceptions. Second, I must also turn myself toward an engagement with that other person. This is part of the dynamic, eternal, and intriguing nature of conflict: It always poses a journey, an encounter with self and with others.

In conflict, whether we are aware of it or not, we are

constantly assessing two sets of questions:

• What are *they* up to? Why are they doing that? What do they need and want? Are they right? Are they good people? How do they really see and feel about me?

• How does it affect *me*? Who am I? Am I right? Am I a good person? What do I need? What am I up to? How do I see and feel about them?

In conflict, we bump up against ourselves and we bump up against others. This is precisely what makes going directly such a complex process. Some of the key steps include these:

First, going directly involves implicit if not explicit self-reflection. Our self-esteem always comes under question. From such a self-encounter, we become aware, an awareness often tainted by our experiences, perceptions, and feelings. Nonetheless, we are aware. In the self-encounter, we make choices about how to respond and engage the opportunity for reflection provided by conflict.

For example, if we are defensive, that usually means we feel insecure. We react to the information coming in and the anxiety it produces. Blaming is often a mechanism for avoiding the anxiety and projecting it onto someone else. If we are to go directly in a constructive way, we need to recognize the task this involves. We must face new information and perceptions, and grapple with the source of our anxieties and fears. We must move *toward* our fears and embrace them in an explicit manner.

Second, in going directly we choose to move toward other people. That often means moving toward the very source of our fears. This is complicated because we will have to do two things at the same time: define ourselves and interact with others. Both pose major challenges and potential pitfalls.

It may be easier for us to move toward others with an attitude of defensiveness, accusation, and blame. Sometimes we may use the more-passive mechanisms of hinting at wrongs but not clarifying the concerns. We may react to their response, counter with better and more rational arguments, and seek to win and show we are right. Or we may retreat and claim it is impossible to deal with that other party.

On the other hand, suppose we wish to go directly in a constructive manner. Then we must both *define ourselves* in a clear, proactive manner and *create the space for interaction* with the perceptions and concerns of the other party. A proactive self-definition in times of conflict is neither blaming nor retreating. It involves a stance of *vulnerable transparency,* where I speak from a depth of awareness about my own concerns, fears, hopes, and needs.

As a wise grandmother once told me in Costa Rica, it is the gift of "going to my enemy with my heart in my hand." Creating a space for interaction is not based on seeking to establish who is right or wrong, or on agreeing and disagreeing. It is basically a stance of connecting with and embracing their experience. It is the gift of recognition and acknowledgment.

I have identified these as social-psychological elements. *Each* also has deep spiritual dimensions. These are perhaps best understood as "disciplines of the soul," to use current terminology. Such disciplines are internal, God-inspired, and God-supported work, necessary for moving toward reconciliation. An initial list of disciplines would include the following:

• *Prayerful vulnerability* means that we dare to look within ourselves, at the sources of our fears and anxieties. We seek understanding that emerges from beyond normal human capacities and responses. Such a discipline can only develop if we understand that conflict provides an opportunity for reflection and growth, even when we feel under siege and threat.

Prayerful vulnerability creates a quality of awareness based on openness to others and God. In that awareness, I can learn about myself rather than defending myself. Instead of seeing myself as superior *to* the other person, I see myself reflected *in* the other, and I find God in both.

In this way, prayerful vulnerability perhaps captures the most proactive elements of Mennonite nonresistance. It is connected to the basic notion of emptying oneself, as Jesus did (Phil. 2:6-7). In the Mennonite tradition, we have defined nonresistance as "not resisting." People tend to take such nonresistance as a negative way and to practice passive avoidance and retreat.

In contrast, prayerful vulnerability as nonresistance implies an active spiritual discipline. It means a willingness to empty oneself, thus creating an awareness about oneself that allows space for God. This leads to internal clarity, openness, honesty, and transparency. These are necessary ingredients for proactive engagement with others, particularly those whom you perceive as threatening. As a discipline of the soul, prayerful vulnerability is a stance of listening and learning.

• *Responsible discernment* happens when we take it upon ourselves to move toward the conflict and others. The nature of this discipline involves the difficult task of identifying clearly when and where we are relationally dealing with a problem. First, if an individual member is to recognize a problem as "sin," we as a church have to prepare for this by working together at discerning what sin is (18:18). Second, at times we fail on the side of letting things go on, expecting others to do this task or not caring about others enough. At other times, we are overly responsible and try to carry everyone's problems on our own shoulders.

Discernment is not simply a thinking process. It is primarily action with others. Disciplined responsibility involves discernment of our accountability and interdependence. Responsible discernment clearly underpins the four steps suggested in Matthew 18.

• *Interactive engagement* is a discipline characterized by both transparency of self and acknowledgment of others. It is not characterized by blaming or retreating. Interactive engagement is a proactive meeting, and readiness for that meeting emerges from within. It permits persons to share their deepest understandings and also interact with those coming from other viewpoints.

Family system theorists counsel us to be a "nonanxious presence," engaged with others without worry or fear (Friedman). John describes this as "perfect love" that can cast out all fear (1 John 4:18). Interactive engagement happens during conflict when we have the spiritual discipline needed for sharing transparently and interacting constructively with experiences, views, and differences that emerge.

I believe that this first step proposed by Jesus—this practice of "going directly"—is central for an understanding of reconciliation. It poses a series of important dual tasks. We must encounter both ourselves and others. We must recognize our fears and yet not be bound by them. We must define ourselves and also acknowledge the experience of others.

Each of these presupposes a significant spiritual dimension of prayerful vulnerability, responsible discernment, and interactive engagement. The required action is summed up in two words, "go directly." Doing that depends on a deeply spiritual and disciplined process.

Step 2: Taking One or Two Witnesses Along

Suppose the erring member does not listen to the counsel of one person, and peace is not restored. Then, Jesus says, the second major step is to involve a broader group of people. These are additional "witnesses," who confirm the evidence. Having two or three means creating a body of people who begin working together to discern what is happening and what needs to be done (cf. 1 Tim. 5:19; Deut. 19:15).

Several points stand out as we look further into this dynamic. The idea of witness carries an image of someone who is present with the people and experiencing the difficulty. In handling conflict and seeking reconciliation, presence involves a twofold stance.

First, the previous discussion asserts that primary *responsibility* lies with those experiencing the conflict. In other words, witnesses help create the forum where reflection, listening, and understanding can emerge. This is different from assessing fault or judging. It points toward capacities for creating a setting where people can be transparent, engage each other, and seek God. By its very nature, such a place can be seen as holy ground. Witnesses need the spiritual disciplines identified earlier and the specific skills related to creating such a space.

A look back across church history, both within and outside Anabaptism, raises an interesting question for us. Have we envisioned and developed the capacities, gifts, and skills necessary for creating such a space and presence? We have generally interpreted this text simply from the operational standpoint of assessing blame and wrong. We have often failed to exercise prayerful vulnerability, responsible discernment, and interactive engagement.

As a result, our outcomes have commonly brought retributive punishment, separation, and distance. We have often based ourselves on "righteousness" in the sense of being "right," not necessarily on holiness, that creates the space for God's presence within each person and between people.

Second, presence gives birth to *accountability* that can only be understood in community. Having witnesses ties the process to broader discernment. Listening and accountability belong to this approach. Accountability is a complicated idea and process. For some, it signals oppression and narrowness, having others tell you what to do, and then always having to be responsible to them. For others, it carries a more positive value. When performed with commitment and mutual submission, accountability brings freedom. We have others to rely on and help us.

At times I have felt both the narrow and the freeing sides of accountability. Yet neither captures the deeper sense of what is happening in this second step. Let me suggest a third option. The phrase "where two or three are gathered" refers to accountability as the *engagement of Truth* that fosters growth in individuals, in their relationship, and in their understanding of God.

When I talk about presence as giving birth to accountability, I do not mean whipping someone back into line or holding fast to dogmatic principles. I refer to a process that creates a space where it is possible to engage *Truth*. This leads us to live by the understanding that emerges from the encounter. Such a process of accountability can ultimately only be understood in community, and it necessarily draws participation from each person involved.

"Two or three gathered" (18:18-20) thus has practical and deep spiritual aspects. On the practical side, this step concerns the development of capacities and skills that help to create a safe space for people to be transparent and interact with each other. The spiritual dimension means that this kind of space is holy ground. It represents the place where we encounter God and each other. This carries us beyond "reaching an agreement and resolving issues." It leads us to deeper understanding and growth as individuals and communities.

Step 3: Telling It to the Church

If the first two steps have not led to a successful conclusion, the third major step in the process is to take the situation to a broader forum, here represented by the word *church*. Take it to the believing community. In the earlier steps, I started by reflecting on social significance before considering spiritual underpinnings. For this step, let me reverse the order, beginning with three basic observations:

First, conflict and church doctrine are connected. How we organize ourselves as churches will affect how we deal with conflict. And how we deal with conflict is reflected in our structures. In the next chapter, I will explore this more when consideration is given to the Jerusalem forum.

Second, working on conflict is spiritual work. This has been discussed earlier in different ways, but here it is seen again. To take the problem to the church assumes a view of the church as a place to process and work with conflict, not a place that is free from conflict.

Third, this simple instruction, "Tell it to the church," offers a model to follow. Reconciliation is the mission of the church. Working on conflict is spiritual. It involves an encounter with ourselves, others, and God. Thus we begin to understand that reconciliation is about the transformation of people and their relationships. It means change, moving from isolation, distance, pain, and fear toward restoration, understanding, and growth. As shown often in the Bible story, the basic purpose of God acting in history is reconciliation. All things are being brought together (Col. 1:20).

At a practical level we can ask ourselves the same questions we did with reference to step 2 (taking witnesses along). How do we make the church community a place where this mission of encounter, growth, and reconciliation can take place? I believe the answer to that question lies in two different but parallel aspects of working with conflict.

Let me reinforce the basic ideas stated in the first two steps. At the practical level, the constructive engagement of conflict at group levels requires the same disciplines that underpin the interpersonal or small-group level. We need self-definition, transparency, and interactive engagement.

What changes in step 3 is the number of people involved. This calls for innovation and creativity in seeking mechanisms for expressing conflict in larger groups, ways that are both responsible and constructive for the people involved. The keys lie in two elements: We need to understand that working with and through conflict is normal, spiritual work. We also need to develop the disciplines and skills to do that work with larger groups of people.

Next we return to our idea of responsible discernment. One of the most difficult tasks facing church leaders is to discern the nature of the conflict. Then they can help develop a forum or process that is appropriate for working it through. Conflicts come in all sizes, depths, breadths, and proportions. It is difficult to find or select the proper procedures for dealing with the nature of a particular conflict.

For example, it may be inappropriate for a committee of four to deal with a certain problem that needs full congregational participation. It may be just as inappropriate to unpack certain personal problems in front of a large group, where more damage than good is done.

Responsible discernment calls for understanding the nature of conflict and for skill in devising appropriate procedures for responding to it. We need a combination of practical skills in dealing with conflict, and we need spiritual disciplines for sustaining and guiding those in the pathway of reconciliation.

In summary, the spiritual dimension of "telling it to the church" lies in a basic understanding. The people who make up the church and its very structure are living testimonies of working out the mission of reconciliation (2 Cor. 5:18-19). The church is a place of encounter. It is a place of Truth-discerning and Truth-telling. It is a place for vulnerable transparency. It is a place for interactive engagement. It is a place of accountability. It is, after all, a place where we journey toward each other and toward God.

Step 4: Relating as with a Gentile and Tax Collector

This is one of the more complicated aspects of the four steps. It has received "no small amount" of practice in church history. What does it mean to treat the person with whom you have not been able to reconcile as a "Gentile and tax collector"? Most church members take this as a mandate for avoiding that sinner. It supposedly provides a license to draw the line and separate ourselves. The erring person becomes someone from whom we need distance.

Let us remember that the first three steps have been oriented to moving *toward* conflict and moving *toward* the other. So I pose the question: How would it be consistent for the last step to mean a movement *away* from both?

I do not have a good answer, but I do have a theological method. My understanding of Anabaptist theology has always meant that we are called to be disciples of Jesus. Theologically, what early Anabaptists emphasized was not formulaic dogmas or basic laws. The focus was on *following* the footsteps of Jesus, an imitation of the behavior and character of Jesus. We are to be centered on Christ, and that is defined largely in terms of action and not simply professed belief.

Ironically, when it comes to conflict, Mennonites are in a peace church tradition but are characterized by a long history of schisms and splits. We tend to split more over matters of practice than over matters of doctrine. To the dismay of outsiders and insiders, we separate over minute details of how we choose to live more than over what we choose to believe. We have disagreed about buttons, bonnets, and buggies, and we have taken those disagreements as serious matters. In our daily living, our beliefs about righteousness are always tested by the "refiner's fire" (Mal. 3:2-3). This carries both strengths and weaknesses.

However, if we take seriously a theology of following Jesus, then we must let Jesus' actions help us understand the steps he outlined. How did Jesus treat Gentiles and tax collectors? In answering that question, we can discover how we should respond when we reach this stage of conflict. What stands out is this simple answer: *Jesus ate with them* (as in Matt. 9:10). Time and again, to the chagrin of Pharisees, Jesus chose the route of seeking out and eating with the very people perceived to be impure and outside the believing community. My interpretation of step 4 is this: *Eat with them!*

"Eating with them" suggests two ideas reflective of what we have seen and what is yet to come in the book:

• Across almost all cultures, eating together implies relationship and connection. "Tables" are what we refer to in the international arena as a metaphor of coming together to talk, negotiate, and seek peace. Eating symbolizes a universal truth that we are connected in the broader human race.

• Eating together puts us on the same level. When we are working in complicated international negotiations, eating together often provides a different way for people to connect with and see each other. When we eat together, we are on the same social plane, we admit our sameness, and we recognize our basic humanity. In this sense, eating is a safe space, a place where we are ourselves.

Now connect the act of "eating together" with the earlier steps. As we reach step 4, Jesus' way of operating is fleshed out. Jesus was clear about who he was and how he saw things. Yet he met people, wherever they were, in ways that showed how his love overcame fear. He sought to build relationships, a way of being connected with others. These are precisely the elements noted in the first two steps. They have a parallel to what is now promoted, two thousand years later, in contemporary family systems theory:

• Define yourself without projection or retreat. Be clear about who you are. Seek vulnerable transparency. Encourage others to do the same.

• Foster a nonanxious presence. Do not get upset, pull back, or be fearful of others when they define themselves differently from you. Interactively engage the difference rather than reacting or trying to control. Move toward the difference and not away from it.

• Maintain relational and emotional contact. Stay connected. Eat with each other.

Step 4 (relating as with a tax collector) poses a challenging dual task for us. Can we clearly define ourselves and still maintain appropriate emotional contact and relationship with those who differ from us or even are our enemies? The answer is never easy. It takes us back to recognizing reconciliation as an encounter both with ourselves and with others.

For church leadership and members, this interpretation guides us in working with issues of church discipline, theological diversity, and ethical misbehavior. We must find the capacities to define ourselves and share what we see and feel. We need to create space for interaction with those who see and feel differently, and promote accountability as the engagement of Truth. We must maintain relationship even when we deeply disagree.

I am frequently asked, "Should we split?" There is

clearly room for going a different direction, and there certainly are times where the most constructive thing needed for reconciliation is time and space. I argue, however, that for the majority of instances, the answer is simple: "No splitting without creating the disciplined holy ground of the three encounters: with self, the other, and God."

Conclusion

A number of important assertions about conflict and how to respond to it begin to emerge from these four steps. They provide the basis of returning to the opening question. How do we understand this window of insight into conflict and reconciliation, as offered by Matthew 18? Here is a short list of declarations, some descriptive and some directive:

1. *Conflict is a part of the church*. What is perhaps most astonishing about the four steps outlined by Jesus is not what he said, but what he assumes and does not say. Jesus simply assumes that in the life of the church, as in the life of any relationship, there will be times of disagreement, conflict, and interpersonal and group clashes.

Jesus moves straight ahead to provide procedure for what we should do as this happens. In this way, Matthew 18 reinforces what we discussed from Genesis 1. Jesus follows a line already established. He assumes the dynamic but often-painful understanding that conflict is a part of human relationships and a part of church life.

2. *Move toward conflict*. What underlies the four steps throughout the Matthew 18 text is Jesus' invitation to move toward the source of our anxiety and toward con-

flict itself. We have a tendency in church circles to see conflict as messy, as "unchristian." We somehow carry an image that the church is a place made up of saints, or at least nice people who do not experience this kind of messiness.

We often set up ourselves to experience a superficial understanding of each other and little positive interaction around our differences. We begin to think that being in church means that we all agree, but the opposite is true.

The church, like the human family, should be a place where members value diversity, encourage honest expression of disagreements, and see relationships as possible between those who do not agree. The church is the place of reconciliation, where conflict is understood as necessary and important for learning and growth. That can happen only as we capture an understanding and vision that moves us toward conflict, not away from it.

3. *Move toward the other.* Jesus challenges us to examine how we view those with whom we experience conflict and deeply felt differences. What consistently underlies the four steps is his call for us to move toward the other rather than away from him or her. We need to cultivate practical skills for confronting each other in better ways. We also need to develop a spiritual discipline through which we seek interactive engagement with others and God.

4. *The church is a forum for expressing and handling conflict.* Jesus provides overall guidelines in this teaching. The church as envisioned here is not simply a glee club of harmonious voices. It is a place to interact with each other, express differences, and work through what may be painful theological and relational issues and concerns. The church is a forum for expressing and dealing with conflict. What is needed is both the vision of integrating conflict as a healthy part of our life and the skills to make it a constructive experience.

5. *The goal of reconciliation is to heal the relationship.* The entire purpose of working through conflict is aimed at bringing back together what has been torn apart through earlier actions, behaviors, and responses. The primary goal is reconciliation, understood as relationship and restoration, the healing of personal and social fabrics. In this process, it is impossible to separate personal from social healing.

Clearly, these are like steps in a journey. It begins with a personal journey within, for the purpose of identifying the source of pain, what is wrong, and understanding it. The process then moves us toward the source of our anxiety and pain that is welling up in the relationship. What rises from this journey is commitment to relationship and interdependence.

Reconciliation here can only be understood in terms of relationship, not in terms of vague, ambiguous, and merely mental processes. Restoration is understood, not as going back to what was, but rather as the image of healing, making a balance, and bringing about what should be. It provides space for growth based on Truth and accountability. In this way, reconciliation is both a process and an outcome.

6. *God is present.* In Matthew 18:20 Jesus says, "Where two or three are gathered in my name, I am there among them." When we recognize that Matthew 18 is dealing with conflict and working toward reconciliation, we comprehend a wholly different interpretation of this verse. "Two or three" does not refer to small numbers of

gathered worshipers. It refers to those who come together to seek healing, restoration, and reconciliation. Verse 20 is a promise: Where you take seriously the mission of reconciliation, I will be present with you.

It is here that we better understand the verses of binding and loosing. Agreeing "on earth about anything you ask" (18:19) is not about the miraculous delivery of "things we want" through prayer. This is especially true in the context of a consumer-driven, product-oriented society. Instead, Jesus reminds us that *the sacred* is present in everyday life. The image drawn in these verses is one that blurs the distinction between the sacred and the profane, or common. I refer here to sacred as the presence of God and of Christ, through the Spirit.

This is similar to the story of the burning bush faced by Moses. Moses turned aside so as not to look directly at the blaze. But God called out, "Come no closer! Remove the sandals from your feet, for the place on which you are standing is holy ground. . . . I am the God of your father" (Exod. 3).

The *sacred* is when and where God is present. I refer to *profane,* not in the sense of using bad language, though that often happens in the midst of heated conflict, but as that which is human and down-to-earth. In terms of our subject matter, there is nothing more profane and common than the normal experience of conflict in the fullness of everyday human interaction.

The paradox is that we rarely see the sacred in the profane, though this is precisely the promise of Jesus. Read these words, remembering that Jesus delivers them in the context of human conflict: "Where two on earth agree, it will thus be agreed in heaven. For where you come together to work on this tough task, I am with you" (Matt. 18:18-20, paraphrased). If we let our eyes see what is not visible on the surface, we capture the image of conflict as holy ground, as the bush in which God is present.

I have always felt that there is nothing more powerful, more moving, and more sacred than when real people, with down-to-earth problems and pain, find reconciliation. Reconciliation goes beyond solving problems, resolving issues, and reaching agreements. It is the process of encounter and healing, of renewed community.

This is the window of Matthew 18. The journey of reconciliation, along the path of conflict, is a journey on holy ground. It is a journey where we meet ourselves, others, and God.

10

KEEPING SILENT AND LISTENING

The story in Acts 15 describes the early church and events surrounding what is often called the Jerusalem Council. Paul and Barnabas have been traveling in foreign territories and sharing the good news of Jesus. They receive dramatic response and then return to the sending church in Antioch of Syria. After calling the church together, they relate "all that God had done with them, and how he [has] opened a door of faith for the Gentiles" (Acts 14:26-28).

However, some folks from Judea arrive and preach to Gentile believers that unless they "are circumcised according to the custom of Moses," they "cannot be saved" (Acts 15:1). The issue produces "no small dissension and debate" between Paul, Barnabas, and the contingent from Judea (15:2). What, exactly, is "no small dissension"? It might better be depicted as a major church fight, a brouhaha in the pews!

I wish we had videotapes of early church meetings and debates. We carry an image of early church leaders as saints and prophets. Yet if we could see them in action in the everyday life of the local congregation, we would likely be shocked. What we would find most startling is how much they are like us, even having sharp disagreements (as also in Acts 15:39). If we had such a video, we would see and hear things not always readily apparent as we read the text.

We would immediately catch the depth of feeling regarding how critical this issue is for the early church. In our day, the question of circumcision as a requirement for membership may seem remote. What lies behind the debate, however, is the much-deeper and more-familiar problem: Do we change our beliefs and practices to assimilate what appear to be new ways that God is moving among us?

They are debating the very identity of those who see themselves as the people of God. We would also hear the voices that we often hear today. Most are filled with concern and deep conviction. Each lays claim to the Truth. Some voices are filled with anger, others with fear. A few carry a message of hope.

Many show ambivalence and confusion. They ask, "If this is true, what is God saying to us?" Others hold fast to what is known, to avoid any confusion or ambiguity. They respond, "Our God is a God of order, clarity, and law." I wonder if you have heard such voices in the midst of church debates:

• "God is calling us to new understandings of who we are and how we should carry out our mission."

• "We have never done it this way. The day you let those people into the church is the day I leave."

• "Look right here in the biblical text. It says clearly that we shall *not* do this."

• "Look right here in the biblical text. It shows how this *can* be done."

Acts 15 is a chapter of conflict. This time we are given a small window into the actual proceedings. How does the early church deal with this problem? Notice again the interplay of practice and spirituality. What steps do they follow? What model does it suggest? What are the assumed spiritual dimensions that undergird such a process?

Principles and Steps for Handling Conflict

Before we look into the broader principles and steps used in Acts 15, we recall two things from this discussion of context. *First,* the conflict poses questions central to both theological and churchly concerns. It has to do with identity, organization, and structure. Who are we? What are we called to? How do we organize ourselves in the world? And who makes these decisions? *Second,* people feel deeply about the issues. Throughout, there are clearly signs of heart-felt emotion. A lot is on the line. With that in mind, let us turn to principles and steps:

1. *Recognize and define the problem.* The story of Acts 15 is extraordinary because of the forthrightness with which the concerns are raised. They do what is not often done in many church conflicts: They start by acknowledging that they have differences and a conflict. I am always amazed at how long "troubles" can brew before anyone is willing to name them.

I have been dealing with church-related conflicts in our denomination over the years. Yet I am always surprised at how many people and congregations will first ask for some general education or training about conflict. It often becomes apparent that beneath the request is a decade-long set of dodged issues and concerns that are about to erupt for the third time in four years.

This first principle operational in Acts 15 has two different but parallel tracks. It is important to understand that there is a significant difference between *knowing* and *acknowledging.* To acknowledge something is to make it explicit, to bring it to the surface, and to recognize it. We are often stuck in a pattern of bumping accidentally into things, going around each other, and circling carefully past the real issues and concerns. This causes confusion and distress. However, we need to openly recognize that we have differences and disagreements that need to be addressed. That step is central to the process of moving forward.

We often fear such acknowledgment. We may fear that, if we openly name the problem, it will separate and damage both our person and our relationship. It will be uncomfortable and painful. The operative base of Acts 15 shows that acknowledging conflict is part of relational transparency and commitment. To disagree does not necessarily have to translate into relational distance and separation. It can mean increased understanding, relationship, and growth.

In my experience, there is once again a paradox: When people fear the step of acknowledgment and avoid it to protect the relationship, those fears often become self-fulfilling. The conflict eventually explodes or implodes. However, if people acknowledge conflict and move toward it early, they find that their relationships can handle even the most difficult of differences.

This paradox lies behind the advice that my colleague Ron Kraybill began to suggest to congregations early in the development of Mennonite Conciliation Service: If you want fewer divisive and church-splitting conflicts, encourage more everyday disagreements in congregational life (Kraybill).

It is equally important to work on defining what the conflict is about. Since this is not a how-to manual for dealing with conflict, I will not go into detail about tools and approaches available for defining conflict. As a principle, however, it is important to understand the purpose. Defining what is going on means locating the conflict, what some people call "mapping" the conflict (Wehr). We want those involved in the conflict to arrive at a common understanding of the nature of the conflict, and of what is necessary to work through the concerns they have.

In international negotiations, this is sometimes called "agenda-building," which can take years. In church settings, a setting is arranged where people can share their concerns with each other and suggest how those concerns could be handled. Often what appear to be the hot issues are actually symptoms of other things happening below the surface, things more difficult to name and pinpoint. In Acts 15, people acknowledge and define the specific concerns that need to be addressed.

2. *Create the appropriate forum for processing matters.* As in Matthew 18, it is necessary to create a forum that fits the needs of the people and the nature of the conflict. This is never an easy task, nor one that appears with ready-made formulas. An orientation toward process is central. How the conflict will be dealt with is of equal or more critical importance than what eventually is decided. Ron Kraybill once quipped, "Process matters more than outcome" (Mennonite Conciliation Service). Or as Jim Laue, a mentor of mine, put it, "If you can trust the process, you can trust the outcome" (Laue and Cormick).

Matters of process are precisely what must be considered when we talk about creating the proper forum. In Acts 15, an implicit but quite astute process orientation is described, built on discernment and creativity. This is a story of recognizing a conflict that needs broad participation. It moves beyond "local" congregational experience and toward an inclusive and extended arena.

We note, for example, the dispute between Paul and Barnabas over the travel schedules and participation of John Mark. That creates sharp disagreement. Rather than convening another Jerusalem Council, they part company (Acts 15:36-41). Presumably this conflict is handled at an interpersonal level, though perhaps not very constructively by the standards of Matthew 18 (cf. the later note of 2 Tim. 4:11).

If we are to take seriously this principle of "creating an appropriate forum," several important characteristics identified as process orientation need to be outlined. *Discernment* emerges from understanding the nature of the conflict and what level of response is needed to deal with it adequately. *Creativity* is needed for flexibility and innovation.

We must consistently find the mechanisms that hold the greatest potential for helping people understand the concerns and constructively meet each other. This calls for an orientation toward involving people in defining the process. It means finding a forum that feels appropriate and placing a high value on participation and ownership in terms of the substance and the process.

3. *Let diverse viewpoints be represented.* One of the most striking aspects of the Jerusalem Council is the careful procedure in letting all viewpoints be aired. It is certainly not a meeting of only those who already agree. Instead, this forum gives space for open expression. People share how God has been moving among them and the differences those experiences have highlighted. Significant leaders are present. People who have never ventured out of Jerusalem are there. Paul and Barnabas come, along with other leaders who are emerging as a result of their ministry.

If we return to the process, we find an operational principle of inclusion. Everyone affected by the decision has a place at the table. I am often reminded of a John McCutcheon song we have played many times at home and on the road:

All God's children have a place in the choir.
Some sing low, some sing higher.
Some sing out loud from a telephone wire.
Others clap their hands, or paws, or anything they got.

This sounds like the Jerusalem Council, but it does not sound like many other church fights. Acts 15, like Genesis 1 and Matthew 18, speaks to the values of diversity, seeking what God is saying to each person, and listening to a voice that can only be fully heard if each is given a place in choir.

4. *Document diversity.* In the Acts 15 story, people are given a chance to talk, from Paul and Barnabas to leaders and the people of Jerusalem. In the mediation field, we refer to this as documenting diversity. It builds on the prior two principles and provides a space for different voices to be heard. Documenting diversity assumes that people *speak and listen.*

To speak well and to listen carefully is no easy task at times of high emotions and deep conflict. People's very identity is under threat. I have the impression it is not that easy in the Jerusalem meeting of Acts 15. Again, I wish we had the video, but we don't. We only have a partially told story. Let us fill it in a bit, looking between the lines.

In the title of this chapter, I touched on a short but very crucial line found in Acts 15:12: "The whole assembly kept silence and listened." From the earlier description, I imagine that there has been a period of interaction. The assembly has probably been loud and somewhat confused, with comments flying past responses and counter-responses.

In other words, this is a meeting like our annual session on the church budget. We argue over why so much money is being spent for a new Sunday school wing rather than for refugees in the Horn of Africa. At a given time, the assembly of Acts 15 "kept silence." This stage is qualitatively different from what has preceded, and that is why the writer emphasizes it.

Documenting diversity in the context of the community is about the task of creating a social space for people to speak and listen, and in so doing to hear the voice of God.

5. *Use the gifts in the community.* As the story weaves on through the meeting, certain people rise and speak. Some bring evidence of what they have seen from their ministry. Some speak of the past. Some speak of how God has worked among them. Some interpret biblical texts. Some formulate ideas of how things will be brought together. Some move the meeting toward a specific outcome. Some write the outcome down. Some carry the message to those not present.

From out of the community come the people and gifts necessary to initiate, support, help create, and sustain the understandings that are reached. This fits Paul's vision of the church as a body (1 Cor. 12–14). He provides a metaphor of different parts that work together. It is a powerful vision that values diversity and seeks common purpose and understanding. The Acts 15 story describes how that works, the creation of a forum that provides for diversity and seeks common understanding.

6. *Decide, then implement decisions.* One of the more striking aspects of the story is the conclusion. It is striking for what it says and what it does not say. We are told that they reach a conclusion, one that marks from now on the development and expansion of Christianity. It is framed as a compromise decision.

In essence, they decide, "We recognize new things that God has envisioned for the church, things that from our tradition we did not expect. We are changing our beliefs to match this new understanding of God moving among us. However, we recognize important things from our past that we must not let go, and we share them explicitly with our brothers and sisters."

This is a firm move to bring closure to the process. There is no "analysis paralysis" or perpetual process, but a specific conclusion that can be implemented.

We are not told what happens at the end of the meeting. I want to know, Does everyone agree with the conclusion? Do they all stay together in harmony? Perhaps some say, "This cannot be. I cannot accept these changes."

We are told that by consent of the body, several leaders are chosen to accompany Paul and Barnabas back to Antioch, to help in reporting the decision of the Jerusalem Council (Acts 15:22-32; cf. 21:25). We are not told who, by that time, has left the church in disagreement.

Does engaging in such a process mean consensus is always reached, that there is full agreement and accord? I can hardly imagine it. Maybe it has happened in Jerusalem. But I guess that there are probably some, maybe just a minority, maybe more, who do part ways. Paul and Barnabas do part company over Mark. Perhaps they also still disagree about whether it is okay for Jewish Christians to eat with Gentile believers (Acts 15:39; 10:28; Gal. 2:13).

If we take seriously the kind of principles identified in Matthew 18, we understand conflict more clearly. We are called as individuals and congregations to learn the disciplines and skills that help us define ourselves, engage each other in nonanxious interaction, and maintain emotional contact even when we disagree.

If that is truly operative here in Acts 15, one can take this kind of stance: "While I do not agree with where you are going, I will not leave the community and thereby try to force you to adopt my way. Let us agree together to stay in relationship, with each of us seeking to be true to what we sense is our different but deepest calling from God. We may part ways in service, but let us maintain fellowship."

Listening: The Spiritual Dimension of Conflict

An important characteristic of dealing with conflict emerges from this story. I will frame it as the spiritual discipline of listening. Beneath the discipline lies a single and most intriguing question: How does God speak to us?

At a technical level, we have often looked at listening in terms of the communication process. One person wants to send a message to another. An intended meaning is thus created that must be conveyed. That meaning is encoded in some fashion, often through words, taking the form of a message. The message must then be perceived by the other person, who decodes it to make sense of it.

Full communication involves the same process in reverse. This purely technical side is already complex. It involves processes of creating, sending, perceiving, and interpreting. If all goes well, what one person means to say is said clearly, and then perceived and interpreted by another in the same way it was intended. That is, we say what we mean, and we understand each other.

We all know that does not always happen, and it certainly becomes much harder to accomplish in the midst of heated conflict. In conflict, before we even hear what the other side has said, we assume we know what they mean. We have already attached motives to their messages. Often, even before they have finished, we are developing our response.

Such dynamics make it difficult to say what we really mean or to hear what the others really mean. We thus create a vicious cycle of misunderstanding and a mutually reinforcing sense of powerlessness. Neither of us feel that we are heard, nor that we say things well. When we do not feel heard, we feel discounted, rejected, and violated. If this continues over time, we are likely to seek ways of making ourselves heard by pushing harder and harder or by retreating for self-protection.

The conflict transformation field teaches that it is necessary to break through this cycle if conflict is to be dealt with constructively (Hocker and Wilmot). Thus we emphasize the need for listening as an art and a skill. Relying heavily on communication and counseling techniques, a primary approach has been to listen at times of conflict, learning the process of applied paraphrasing, or "active listening."

Active listening is a practical and useful method. As an applied technique, paraphrasing means to repeat in your own words what another person has said. This changes the dynamics of communication. It slows us down a bit. We check whether what we heard the other person say is what they really meant, and whether what they meant is what we have understood. We show the other that we are truly interested in understanding them and in being understood.

Instead of relying on instinct and gut reaction, in paraphrasing we actively try to break out of the cycle of miscommunication. We must first make sure we have understood each other before we try to deal with our differences.

I have monitored this process. When paraphrasing is a natural part of a person's repertoire of skills and when it is done well, it goes virtually unperceived. People want to be heard and are often grateful that somebody cares enough to interact constructively with what they are saying.

However, I have also found that when we teach the skill in seminars, there is some reaction against the technical skill. People dislike any formulaic crutch that becomes part of the technique: "What I hear you saying is . . ." It makes the process sound fake. People react against being submitted to a form of gratuitous parroting, or cheap "psychologizing."

This reaction leads to an insight that helps us connect to a deeper level. What really bothers people is the perception of underlying purpose and attitude. The technique is merely a tool. It can be used for good or bad. What counts is intuited beneath the technique: the quality and nature of one's spirit. True listening is connected to a spiritual process. Consider three different but related facets of this deeper process.

1. *Listening is a spiritual discipline.* Listening as a technique takes art and skill. To apply the technique takes discipline. But such technical discipline, even if well-honed in the helping professions, does not in itself lead to a deeper level of genuine listening. I can use the technique, for example, to simply get information about you. What leads to the deeper level is whether I *interact* with you as a person about whom I *care*.

To use a more biblical term, listening is a spiritual discipline if, like a spring, it bubbles up from genuine love. I refer to love in the sense of *agape*, a self-sacrificing love, which today is better understood as true *caring*. I take care in my relationship with you. I care about your experience and journey. I care about you as a person. This involves personal risk. In actively caring and seeking to truly interact with you, my experience and journey will be affected, shaped, and molded. I will learn something of you and something of me.

2. *Listening is like prayer.* Now add a second intriguing idea. The pursuit of listening as a spiritual discipline calls for re-framing what we are doing when we listen. Re-framing is based on the idea that we create meaning when we associate things together, and different associations provide different meanings (Watzlawick, Weakland, and Fisch).

I have often used my son's response to "babysitting" as an example. When his older sister Angie was in school, Joshua was dropped off a few hours a week at a neighbor's house. He was negative about the experience. If we referred to this as "going to the babysitter's place," he rebelled. Babysitting meant being left out, going to a stranger's house, or whatever image was conjured up in his four-year-old mind.

To deal with his resistance, we tried referring to this

time and place as "school," and to the babysitter as a teacher. Then Joshua associated it with what his big sister was doing, and he was content. It had a positive meaning. The same thing meant something different because of its different connections.

The same is true of listening. Much of what is technically taught about listening is associated with professional fields. We have, I think, relied on a narrow and unnecessarily superficial association. It therefore is not surprising that we understand listening primarily as a technique. I believe prayer is the closest biblical and spiritual phenomenon to listening. The purpose of this chapter is not to explore and fully unpack all that might be meant by prayer. However, there are a number of characteristics to consider, particularly in the context of thinking about conflict and reconciliation.

I understand prayer to involve a relationship and conversation with God. It is ongoing. I take what occupies my mind and heart, and I seek to learn what God has for me. The latter can only be discovered through a process of learning. I must bracket the many noises and rumblings that float through my mind and my busy day. I do this so I can focus and make it possible for God's voice to enter and speak, and for me to recognize God's voice.

This involves an attitude of attentive awareness and a discipline. In attentive awareness, I pay attention and look for the presence of God in what may appear to be the most mundane of things. Discipline implies that it takes consistent willingness. I must care about doing it or it doesn't happen.

The desire for relationship and love supports attentive awareness and discipline. Prayer is not so much about words or formulas. Prayer is attentive awareness and discipline based on relationship and love. This combination creates the space for interaction, transparency, and understanding. When we practice these things, we are truly listening.

3. *Listening is seeking God.* The idea of prayer and listening as a spiritual discipline leads to the discovery that to truly listen is to seek God. This is rather astonishing, given that we are exploring the context of how we understand conflict. Situations of conflict are often filled with noise and periods of deep, silent distance. How is it possible in these situations to find God? How can listening to my enemy be understood as sacred? It involves at least a twofold process.

First, from earlier discussions in Genesis, I begin with a view that there is "that of God" in every human being (see chapter 8, above). Second, God moves and speaks to each of us, whether we are aware of it or not. This leads to a simple but profound conclusion. We provide the space to listen to another and genuinely try to understand. Thus we are helping to create the opportunity for that person and for ourselves to get in touch with what God may be saying and what God is trying to do in the present.

I have referred to this as "prophetic listening," a concept I first heard from Elise Boulding. During conflicts, many prophets speak and often quite loudly. People lay claim to the Truth as if it were theirs alone. Few prophets listen. Prophetic listening, as I see it, is the discipline of listening with others in such a way that it helps them get in touch with what God is telling them (cf. 1 Cor. 14:29; 1 Thess. 5:20-21).

In this sense, prophetic listening is like going on a journey alongside the person to whom we are listening.

This kind of listening does what few other things can do. It helps us feel the presence and direction of God's Truth.

Conclusion

All of this has profound implications for how to think about and respond to conflict at all levels, but especially for church-related dissension and debate, large or small. When we understand listening as a spiritual discipline, as prayer and seeking God, then we recognize that God speaks to us through others.

Our capacity to listen to God is only as great as our capacity to listen to each other when we are in conflict. I mean that literally. We test our real capability to listen, not when it is easy, but when it is most difficult. Listening is much more than a technique devised to improve communication. Listening is about the process of relationship, engaging Truth, and finding God.

The churchly importance imbedded in Acts 15 cannot be overstated. The procedures of Acts 15 give us a vision that the beloved community is not a static outcome of our work. It is a dynamic process of interaction and growth. Conflict is not and cannot be seen as a disruption in our otherwise peaceful life. Conflict provides an arena for revelation.

Reconciliation is understood as both a place we are trying to reach and the journey that we take up with each other. The window of Acts 15 gives a living model of this idea. Conflict provides an arena for God to speak. This can happen as we understand listening to be a spiritual discipline, like prayer, and place ourselves into a journey of seeking God together.

PART 3

THE CALL TO RECONCILIATION

WHEN ALL THINGS COME TOGETHER

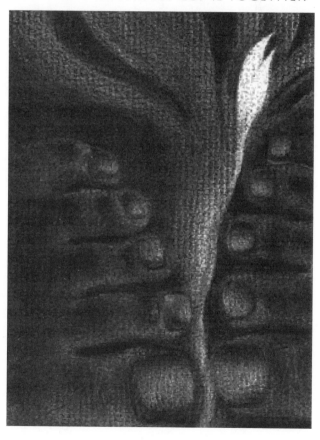

11

THE MINISTRY
OF RECONCILIATION

My colleague at Eastern Mennonite University recalled a conversation with several members of one of our constituent congregations. They had asked, "When will the Mennonite Church and its academic centers stop fussing so much about peace and justice issues and get on with the gospel?"

My colleague wanted to know, "How would you answer these genuine concerns?"

"I may not be a good person to ask that," I replied, feeling my heart skip a beat as I heard the question, "because my first response is that reconciliation *is* the gospel."

The Purpose of God's Mission

In earlier chapters and through a variety of stories, I have said that reconciliation is a journey toward a place where Truth, Mercy, Justice, and Peace meet. On this journey we encounter God, others, and ourselves. Such a journey, I believe, is the essence of the gospel. It lies at the heart of God's intention for humanity and with humanity.

In Christian circles, we have too often assumed that reconciliation is an outgrowth, a side benefit that emerges from the core of individual faith, confession, and conversion. In this view, reconciliation is a *product* of proper belief. However, I maintain that reconciliation is better understood as a journey.

In these concluding chapters, I want to clarify that an

understanding of reconciliation as a journey will require us to adjust our thinking and activity. To see reconciliation as a *journey* and not a by-product means that reconciliation is central, a defining model of *who* and *how* God is in the world.

I view reconciliation as *the* mission, the organizing purpose around which we understand and see God's work in history. I believe that the way God has chosen to be present and act throughout history demonstrates a methodology of reconciliation. *Our mission* is to align ourselves with God, who is working to bring all things together, to *reconcile* all of creation and particularly a broken, estranged humanity. This is the "universal restoration" destined to bless all families of the earth (Acts 3:20-26; Col. 1:20).

The *methodology* is about how God's mission is made present in our world: It happens through the incarnation, the way in which Word becomes flesh. This is why building peace, justice, and reconciliation is not a sideshow interest for a few. Reconciliation is getting to the heart of the gospel and getting on with the gospel.

I believe the journey of reconciliation is embodied in Christ, God's Son, the one who creates the space that brings people and things together. As followers of Christ, we are called to align ourselves with this mission and methodology, to embody God's reconciling love and make it present in the world. Both the mission and the methodology return to the powerful imagery of a journey. Mission is an act of moving toward, sending, and going. Methodology is about *how* such a journey takes place.

From the eyes of faith, the truly defining moments in history are the points where God moves toward us, an estranged and broken people, to restore and heal what has been torn apart. Ultimately, words cannot accomplish this mission. New teachings coming from God and delivered as guidelines are not enough. It was not enough for God to send voice pieces, the prophets (Heb. 1:1-2). In the end, this journey requires the giving of God's self. The Word becomes flesh (John 1:14).

God in the form of Jesus sets up his house beside us so that we see, hear, feel, touch, and interact with a person who walks and lives with us. Through Jesus, we see that God's reconciling love is made present. It takes the form of one who embodies true love and dares to live a dream that it is possible to reconcile all things.

Here I reflect on the nature of this journey and the quality of God's love. I will work with the Pauline vision of Christ, who through the cross has brought all things together.

All Things Come Together

In the letter to the Colossians, Paul writes that through Christ, God was pleased to reconcile all things to himself, and that in Christ all things are held together (Col. 1:17, 20). To the Ephesians, he writes that through the cross, Christ has broken down the dividing wall of hostility and created in himself a new humanity that is reconciled with each other and God (Eph. 2:13-14).

We have generally understood this language as a theological treatise about *atonement,* which then leads to a *holy* life. We tend to see atonement as an act of sacrifice whereby Jesus' death on the cross satisfies our debt of sin in front of God our Creator. As such, atonement is understood as a ritualistic act of cleansing, often individualized to the relationship between a person and God: Through the blood of Christ on the cross, an indebted, sinful person is reconciled to God. Holiness then apparently means keeping ourselves pure, at some distance from whatever is messy, evil, and sinful.

Ironically, this construct lends itself to a narrow understanding, not only of atonement and holiness, but of the very nature of God's mission. Let us expand our view by using the bold and venturesome vision of Paul. He states in simple terms that God's purpose and mission is to bring "all things together." This is a vision of reconciliation. It lies at the heart of the good news. God moves toward us to mend and heal what has been torn apart. God's mission is reconciliation.

As a point of departure and reference, this vision changes our understanding of atonement and holiness. It provokes us to reassess and develop a more challenging way of thinking about mission, our place in the world, and our part in the work of God in history.

In the Pauline vision, atonement does not simply mean a sacrifice that satisfies an individual debt. There is a greater emphasis on atonement as a personal, social, and political *process* of reconciliation and healing. Holiness is not driven by a concern for boundaries that protect purity. Instead, holiness is carried out through people who embody the reconciling love of God and take up residence in real-life problems and relationships, with all the ambiguities they bring.

Let us explore this vision in more detail by reconsidering Ephesians 2:11-22 with the lenses of reconciliation as mission placed over our eyes. Paul describes two peoples who have been divided and estranged. And then he writes,

> But now in Christ Jesus you who once were far off have been brought near by the blood of Christ. For he is our

peace; in his flesh he has made both groups into one
and has broken down the dividing wall, that is, the
hostility between us. He has abolished the law with its
commandments and ordinances, that he might create
in himself one new humanity in place of the two, thus
making peace, and might reconcile both groups to God
in one body through the cross, thus putting to death
that hostility through it. (Eph. 2:13-16)

Paul starts with a reference to peoples who are separated, enemies, distant, strangers who stand apart.
Through Christ, however, the dividing wall of hostility
has been broken down. *In Christ,* those who once were
enemies are now reconciled in a new, single humanity. I
note here two qualities, neither of which is particularly
ritualistic or symbolic. On the contrary, they are rather
literal and organic.

First, Paul makes reference throughout the text to peoples who are enemies. The context to which he refers is
that of the Jews and Gentiles, enemy peoples not unlike
the Serbs and Croats, the Hutus and Tutsis, or the First
Nations and the Americans of European descent. These
are people who have hurt and killed each other, whose
identities are sharply divided by a sense of threat, injustice, and separation. Throughout the text, these are referred to as *groups* and not as individuals. This is so true
that the concluding reconciliation creates a new humanity by bringing the groups together.

In this text, atonement is literally about a dynamic
group process, a journey where real enemies with deep
hostilities are reconciled. Organically, Christ is plowing
soil where seeds and roots of hatred have been born and
fed for centuries. Joe Campbell, my good colleague from
Northern Ireland, commented, "We must tend to our

soil that produces the bitterness and anger." This is simultaneously a personal, social, and political process. It is not, however, merely an individualistic event.

Second, Paul depicts Christ as a person through whom new relationships are formed. Again I am struck with the literal and organic nature of this description. In the life of Jesus, holiness is defined more than anything else by his *persistent movement toward* people, their pain, and the formation of a new relationship.

In this text, Paul declares that through Christ, through a person who reaches out across lines of hostility, through his very flesh and person, enemies meet and are held together. Thus they form a new humanity, a new relationship. What we find here is the most necessary part of the mission methodology: movement into *relationship.*

From the perspective of God's purpose, the example of Christ Jesus is clear. It is not possible to pursue reconciliation except through people who risk the journey to relate across the social divides. Thereby they help make present the reconciling love of God. In other words, through people who reach across the lines of hostility, a new relationship between enemies becomes possible.

Let us return for a moment to the Mennonite ethos and practice mentioned earlier. In practical terms, over past centuries we have chosen to embody atonement and holiness by the motto "We are in the world but not of the world" (see John 17:11, 16, KJV). We use this text to support notions of nonconformity. We say this means that we choose not to live conformed to the pressures around us but rather by the standards and ethics of the kingdom of God (cf. Rom. 12:2).

In practice, this has often been applied as removing ourselves from the world, pulling back, and isolating our communities from the world. Because of our concern for holiness, we try to control the environment around us so that we will have less tendency and opportunity to fall and fail. In our practice we have placed the emphasis on the *"not of the world"* portion of the motto.

Ironically, God through Jesus seems to have approached holiness and atonement with an emphasis on the *"in the world"* part of the motto. The world is a messy, violent, and broken place. God's model Child, Jesus, was needed *in the world*, to provide the distinctive direction. This would be something different from the way people were acting and carrying on. By God's example through Jesus, "to be in but not of the world" means that we move toward human troubles and choose to live in the messiness. That way the alternative of God's reconciling love can be made known.

From such a view, atonement and holiness are not about establishing proper ritual and merely maintaining individual purity. Atonement and holiness are about entering relationships and starting dynamic social processes that help create the space for a new humanity to emerge. We choose to journey toward and with those who have experienced the deepest division and separation because this is God's mission and Christ's example.

Conclusion

I believe the Pauline vision leads us to a simple but challenging conclusion: God is working to bring all things together. The purpose is to heal and to reconcile people with each other and with God. God's mission is also ours. *We* have been given the same ministry of reconciliation (2 Cor. 5:18-20).

This ministry, as articulated by Paul, is not just about

individual salvation. It is about facing divisions and re-storing people in their relationships with others and with God. It is about joining God in the mission of reconcil-iation by building bridges and bringing down the divid-ing walls of hostility between individuals and groups.

True atonement and holiness place us in the journey to make real the reconciling love of God in our lives and to heal our broken communities across the globe. Our mission is to walk the path by which all things come to-gether.

12

THROUGH THE VALLEY AND TO THE TABLE

Through the lens of Psalm 23, I want to look at the methodology of this mission, the journey toward reconciliation. Most of us learned this psalm as a child. What I remember is the emphasis placed on the *Shepherd* metaphor. God, the Shepherd, is my guide and protector for times when I am afraid or under duress.

I thought of a God who was there when the lights went out at night and my mind played games. What threatening things might be lurking in the dark! I am sure that this psalm is still useful in all those specific ways. I still believe it is deeply connected to fear and moving through fear.

In recent years, however, I have begun to see further light in this psalm. I now take it as a briefly stated ethic for reconciliation, nonviolence, and peacebuilding.

Walking with the Shepherd

Understanding Psalm 23 as an ethic for reconciliation started for me through experiences I had in settings of extreme violence and war. On various occasions, I have found myself under psychological pressure and physical threat, living with fear all around me and within me. This psalm was always one of the texts I came back to in my mind when I felt pressure and fear mounting.

The words were the same as when I was a child. Yet the context of reading them in the midst of war and violence, where my friends and family were under the threat of losing their lives, drew forth new meanings. Things started to jump out at me from the psalmist's writing. In these six verses, I saw an intriguing mix of images. At times the verses create visual pictures that seem almost contradictory. Nevertheless, they always return to a central theme.

The theme of the psalm is clearly that of *a journey* through fear and a radical nonviolent reliance on God. I believe this is the method chosen by God and embodied in Jesus' life here on earth. From working in settings of deep-rooted violence and war, I now read Psalm 23 in three distinct blocks: The Preparation and Restoration, the Valley, and the Table.

Preparation and Restoration

In the first lines we find the imagery of the Shepherd and the provision of all we need, which restores the soul. If we rely on the opening lines, we might assume that restoration and "right paths" are somehow connected to "green pastures," gently flowing streams, and an abundant life free of basic worries. Those needs are abundantly met. In other words, the opening image is this: God is good. God provides. God leads us through a life of beauty and fulfillment.

The irony of all six verses in Psalm 23, however, is found in how one image is juxtaposed with a contrasting one. At first we seem to know where the psalmist is going. Then we are surprised to find ourselves located in a different place than where we expected to be. This is the tension we feel as we move between the place where the Lord *restores* our soul, and the walk toward and along the paths of *righteousness* (KJV).

We can only understand the jump between these two places as we attach "paths of righteousness" to the next lines. These are not plush and easy paths. They are tough trails and dark valleys that lead us toward *the enemy*.

I have always found that reading biblical texts in different languages adds new dimensions and meanings. In this case I was struck repeatedly with how Spanish versions of Psalm 23 would talk about *"just* paths" and "paths of *justice."* When we understand that *justice* is the trail we are entering, then we are invited to reconsider what the green pastures and restoration of the soul may mean.

The psalm does not simply represent a carefree attitude: "Don't worry; the Shepherd will take care of all your needs." The psalmist says that the Shepherd is preparing us to follow him on a journey. Green pastures is the work of holiness. They represent the inner agenda of our own needs and fears. We seek a place of inner security that will enable us to face the anxiety likely to emerge as we walk the coming path.

From this perspective, green pastures, still waters, and a restored soul reflect the kind of work necessary to sustain ourselves as we take up the journey down the path of justice. This preparation requires us to overcome our fears. We are, after all, led by the Shepherd and by the Son, who is the Good Shepherd (John 10:11). Restoration is the starting point. The psalm prepares us to walk and follow.

The Valley

The *valley* then depicts the nature of this walk for justice. The Shepherd takes us immediately into the messy valley of the shadow of death. We face here our greatest fears and those who produce fear in us. Yet, the psalmist says, we "fear no evil." This statement is especially intriguing since it does not say we do not fear; it says we do not fear evil.

Here the image created pulls us to move toward and engage the very things that produce fear in us. We are not worried that we will be contaminated in the process. We are free to engage, relate, and interact with the people and challenges we meet on this trail of justice and righteousness. We are freed of anxiety that we will be overwhelmed by evil. In fact, the opposite is true: We are confident that even though we do not know what will come along the trail, we know that the Shepherd will lead. We are asked to walk and follow.

Here again, we meet the paradoxes of this psalm. We go into the place that is most dangerous, not flinching from what produces the fear. We are even comfortable to interact with the messiness, because here we find God. This is the significance of the declaration, "You are with me; your rod and staff—they comfort me."

Take note that our lack of anxiety is not due to our self-defense or protection that comes from our physical or intellectual force, capacity, or power to defend. It is our defenselessness and not knowing that creates a radical nonviolent dependence on God. We are assured because we are confident that we walk in the presence of God. We recall Jesus' promise in Matthew 18: "To those who take seriously the journey of reconciliation, I am with you" (paraphrased).

In many ways the valley represents our stepping by faith into the stream of our own fears and into the messiness of a violent world, dependent on and following the Shepherd. That Shepherd is forever leading us *into the world.* But always we are with a presence that creates something different, new possibilities, redemptive seeds pregnant with change for us and them. With the Shepherd, we are fearful but not anxious.

The Table

In the midst of this valley, we find a table prepared in the presence of our enemies. The psalmist sets the image of a table alongside the presence of enemies. This is an interesting mix of metaphors, an unexpected juxtaposition.

If we are talking about a "negotiation" table, it could make sense that enemies are present. However, this does not seem to be the understanding. What seems implicit, once again, is the idea of restoration in the presence of threat. Consider for a moment each aspect of the clause: "You prepare a table before me in the presence of my enemies."

A table is a symbol of food, nourishment, relationship, and communion. Around the table families and communities gather. It is a place where common humanity is engaged at its fullest, a place where basic needs are met and relationships nurtured. In my own family experience, both immediate and extended, the table is a gathering place where our lives intersect, where the day's activities are prepared and recounted. It is a place, perhaps like none other, where we are just ourselves, without pretense and without fear. The table is the safest family space we share.

In this sense, the table is restoration, a place where things are brought back together. The French word for an eating establishment, now commonly used worldwide, is *restaurant,* a place to restore and replenish. The psalmist claims that as we walk this path of justice into the valleys of darkness, a table is prepared for us. It is a place where we can be nourished, restored, and connected with others. A place where we can be without pretense or fear. A place in which to be ourselves.

Then, in nearly the same breath, we are told this is also a place where we encounter the enemy. The enemy conjures up images of fear, threat, and death. It represents all that stands in our way, that wishes to do us harm. Unlike the table, the enemy creates a place of anxiety and hostility, a place where it is not safe to be ourselves. The enemy creates a space where we feel a need to protect, to hide, and to disconnect.

The intriguing aspect of Psalm 23 is how these two contradictory energies are held together at the same time, in the same sentence, in the same breath. The psalmist declares that we are led in the paths of justice. We meet the enemy in such a way that we are simply and fully ourselves, without pretense or fear of contamination. This is no ordinary journey. This is not a common path. This is not just any table. This is the path and table that embrace the reconciling encounter.

Conclusion

The result of the Psalm 23 journey is again strikingly ironic. If we follow the Shepherd through the valley of encounters, we will be blessed. Goodness and mercy shall follow. We will live in the house of the Lord. We come full circle back to where we started. These are the images we find in this extraordinary vignette of reconciliation.

The Lord's house starts with the beauty of green pastures and still waters, the inner preparation and soulful restoration necessary to take up the journey. We know the Shepherd. He takes us down the path of justice and moves us toward and into the messiness of the world. Led by that Shepherd, we are dependent not on our strength and power, but on the protection and guidance of God.

We walk, without fear of contamination, to a place of encounter where we sit at a table and eat with the enemy. From this journey along the path of justice, we come to mercy and goodness and a restored soul.

13

WANDER, WONDER, AND WAIT

In the spring of 1997, I sat across the table from a good friend and dear sister, Rose Barmasai. She had brought her team of colleagues from the Kenyan National Council of Churches Peace Initiative to a meeting with me in Nairobi. For several years they had been diligently working, at considerable risk to themselves, in areas of their home country where ethnic groups were clashing with each other.

Our conversation began with discussions about strategies for building peace and reconciliation in settings of violence. A single question kept cropping up. "We do all these good things. We engage in these workshops. We build relationships. We work with the pastors," they said. "Yet every time we think we are making a step forward, something happens that puts it all back to zero again. How do we sustain hope in the face of everything falling apart?"

The Journey Through Disillusionment

Only a few months earlier, I had been with our colleagues in Nicaragua, Zoilamerica Narvaez and Alejandro Bendaña. As explained earlier, they work extensively in a reconciliation project that brings together former enemies, fighters from both sides of the war. They had been working at this initiative for more than seven years and had made tremendous progress. However, the elections were coming, and tensions were increasing as the days passed. I can still hear the heavy feeling of concern and anguish from those conversations. "We are going to lose so much if people go back to fighting. How are we to keep going?"

At about the same time, I received an invitation from Corrymeela in Northern Ireland. This ecumenical center brings together Protestant and Catholic religious and lay leaders from across the island. They provide a critical and unique place for people to meet and develop relationships that cut across the deep divide separating the two communities.

At this stage in the Irish peace process, people had their hopes raised when various paramilitary groups declared cease-fires. They had watched the opening of the peace talks and the promises that maybe at long last the sought-for peace would come to that land each community calls home. But those high hopes were dismally dashed in following months by the renewal of violence and the collapse of talks into political stalemate.

The letter from Corrymeela laid out a simple request. "We find ourselves facing hopelessness and feel a need to explore our common experience of disillusionment. We would like you to help us think about how people of faith move *Through Disillusionment.*" The last two words became the title of the weekend seminar for religious leaders from both sides.

"What," I asked myself, "do I say about sustaining hope?" When I look back across the twenty-some years that I have worked in this field, I must confess that precious little has been accomplished in ways that we could call definitive "results." So much of what I do in supporting efforts for reconciliation is slow and ongoing. I experience many tiny steps forward and then big steps backward.

The hardest part of my job is responding to well-meaning questions from my home congregation when I return from a trip. "How did it go? Was it successful? Do you feel like something was accomplished?"

I find myself skirting the real question. "It was good trip. I work with great people, but they have a real mess on their hands. They are facing a long, hard road ahead."

What I am implying is something more bleak, but I do not want admit it out loud: Deep down inside, I have no idea whether these past two weeks of extremely intense discussions and training will make any impact on that situation of violent conflict. It has been raging for years, in some cases longer than I have been alive.

It is hard to explain that much of what we do can perhaps only be measured across a decade or even a lifetime or more. I am arriving at a conclusion that I shared with the participants at Corrymeela. Increasingly, I see the journey toward reconciliation as characterized by the willingness to wander, wonder, and wait.

Wander

My first recollection of the word *wander* comes from the song we used to sing in elementary school: "I love to go a-wandering, along the mountain track." It always left me with a sense of adventure and simply enjoying the beauty of whatever appeared along the path. There is an aimlessness to wandering. It means to take up a trail without a clear destination marking the reason for the journey.

This is how many faith journeys in the Bible are described. The most specific would be that of Abraham, who set out on a journey without knowing the exact destination. The Lord told him to go "to the land that I will show you" (Gen. 12:1). His was the call to a journey that required faith. He faced forward and walked without knowledge of exactly where he was going or what would happen along the way. This became a permanent and lifelong journey for him.

Abraham's journey is a metaphor of faithful wandering for all believers who are "looking for" the community being built by God, the "city that is to come" (Heb. 11:8-10; 13:14). To wander is start the journey, not driven by an obsession for reaching the destination as the measure of success, but rather by the conviction that we are called to walk this path.

Wandering is linked with the idea of the *stranger,* often used in the Bible to describe people of faith sojourning in a foreign land, as did Abraham (Heb. 11:9). The people of God are repeatedly reminded to be generous and welcome the stranger in their own land, because they once were strangers in a foreign land (as in Deut. 10:18-19; Heb. 11:13; 13:2).

A stranger has special qualities. Who one is and what one seeks is not known and shared by those around you. In living as strangers, we redo the experience of Israel, who wandered for forty years in the desert. We should not lose sight of the fact that forty years means four decades, a full generation.

As I look at my own experiences on the journey toward reconciliation, they have the qualities of wandering. The desert in which I travel is the pain and anger produced from violence, division, hatred, and a sense of injustice that runs deep across generations.

When I set out on the journey of reconciliation, I choose to walk with people into and through that desert. It involves wandering alongside those who are entering the valley of the shadow of death. They spend a lifetime feeling like strangers who seek understanding. They struggle with complex dilemmas and constant disappointments. They walk on a pathway that appears to go in endless circles.

I am reminded of a recent trip to Colombia. I have been collaborating with Justapaz, a center for nonviolence and conflict resolution established as a form of ministry by the Mennonite Church in Bogota. The director of Justapaz is Ricardo Esquivia, who has worked for years to transform the violence of more than forty years of war into a just and lasting peace in his native country.

As part of that effort, we have begun a series of training courses on peacebuilding focused on the Colombian conflict. Participants in the training program have included every sector and level of Colombian society, from government figures to universities and local churches.

The seminars were soon transformed into projects to implement the ideas presented in the workshops. In 1997 one of the government ministries asked Justapaz to help facilitate a design for peacebuilding in one of the most violent regions of the country. The working group to design the strategy would include representatives from several branches of the government, the National Human Rights office, the military, and three Mennonites. With a combination of excitement, fear, and adventure, Ricardo, Paul Stucky, and I wandered into the role of leading the design workshop.

The first day went well. We were a diverse group, with public figures, government functionaries, military officials, and devout pacifists. Yet we all had same the driving question before us: How do we impact the level of violence in rural Colombia in a way that can be clear, sustained, and creative?

Sometime during that first night, however, an unexpected twist arrived that had nothing to do directly with our seminar. A group of paramilitaries entered and brutally attacked a human rights worker and his family in their private home. The husband, the wife, and the father were all killed in cold blood. They had hidden their infant son in a drawer of a dresser, and he survived. The family members were friends and colleagues of Ricardo, Paul Stucky, and the Human Rights officers attending our meeting.

Early the next day, before our meeting started, Ricardo and I walked to the funeral home where the caskets held the bodies. We sat there in silence for a long time. Then we walked toward our meeting. As we left, I remember Ricardo talking and talking, as if he needed to get things out. "But for the grace of God," he would say, "there go I. How long will this go on? How long before this country can once again value the preciousness of life?

"You know," he told me, "last week Patricia and I happened across our wedding picture. It startled us to realize that most of the friends who accompanied us that day are now gone. Dead! Killed! But I believe that God has given us these experiences for a reason. Ours is not to get lost and perplexed in the questions. Ours is to be faithful. Our day is coming," he said several times. "Our day is coming."

We walked on toward our meeting. Back we went into the discussions of how to build peace with this working group made up of people who were not like-minded. By the nature of their jobs, some of them were close to the very people who had committed those atrocities.

This is the lesson about wandering for reconciliation that I have learned from Justapaz and Ricardo in Colombia. Wandering means taking up a lifelong journey without knowing what the exact destination will be. We only know that God places before us a path filled with personal challenges and setbacks, opportunities, and people.

Wonder

To wonder is to be perplexed, curious, and intrigued. We are filled with childlike amazement at how things are and why they are that way. We set ourselves to investigating, poking around, and figuring things out.

Those who wonder live with inquisitive minds, as did Martin Hofkamp. Some years ago, his parents, Mike and Becky, were on Mennonite Central Committee assignment in the Philippines. When I stayed with them, Martin was just starting his first experience of school. At supper he would entertain us with endless questions: "Why . . . ? Why . . . ?"

"Why do we eat mangoes, Daddy?" he would ask.

"Because they taste good," Mike would say.

"Why do they taste good?"

"Because God made them that way."

"Why did God make them?"

One day the teacher sent home a special certificate for Martin. He had received the "Why-Because" award. To wonder is to fill ourselves with such a curiosity.

To wonder is to be naive. I have decided that, unlike the common assumption, naïveté is not a negative thing. It is good. I have looked back across my own learning in this field of peacebuilding and reflected on results. I am amazed at how much of what I knew and the techniques I had mastered were not the keys to what I consider my greatest accomplishments. For the most part, the best things happened because I did not know and therefore was naive.

These past few years, I have started a special journal where I am writing out what I think are pieces in a future book. The working title is this: *Divine Naïveté: Stories of How Being Naive Accomplished More Than Being Smart.* It will be filled with anecdotes of the times and places where not knowing and actual stumbling led to important insights, understandings, and breakthroughs.

To wonder, to be naive, means choosing to live in a permanent state of ambiguity. Wondering requires us to raise our capacity to live without final and complete answers and to withdraw from quick, easy, and pat solutions. When we wonder, we suspend immediate judgment. More than anything else, wondering requires us to recognize that we do not know, and therefore we must seek to find out.

Hence, wondering is not about being stupid. It is about living with enough humility that we continue to seek for understanding. Many times I am struck with how easy it is to act like I know the answer and how hard it is to reach that place of honesty where I can say, "I don't know." But these are precisely the elements we need to become seekers of Truth.

In the end, wondering sustains the journey toward Truth. Truth requires not that we consider ourselves as perfect, as knowing it all. Truth requires that we maintain a fundamental belief that there is more and deeper understanding to be gained. We see our lives and work, Gandhi said, as a continuing set of experiments in Truth (Gandhi). Thus we recognize that we must rely on something that goes beyond our individual capacity.

Arrogance appears when we believe we are above others, independent, relying only on ourselves. Arrogance is the opposite quality from wondering. When we wonder, we keep looking, seeking, and seeing ourselves in relationship with others and God. We recognize that we need them to gain insight into Truth.

In the journey toward reconciliation, wondering helps us see ourselves not as experts who have arrived with final answers, but as travelers with others seeking to understand. One of my most daunting challenges comes when students and participants return after a year of working with serious conflict situations. They tell me, "You know that idea and strategy you talked about last year in the workshop? Well, we tried it and it didn't work. So we thought of another idea and tried that. It didn't work either."

I also hear myself saying, "Well, there are these people I know in a situation that is somewhat like yours, and they tried this other idea. Now it didn't exactly work out like they thought, but . . ."

The conversation goes on, not filled with words of solutions but with our seeking to understand together, to find the next step on the journey. To wonder keeps our eyes, ears, and minds alive to the constant process of discovery, learning, and Truth.

Wait

In peacebuilding I have discovered that, more than anything else, I have had to learn, relearn, and remind myself to learn about waiting. I wait for good ideas to come. I wait for ideas to take hold. I wait for understanding. I wait for seeds to mature and grow. I wait for change. I wait for people to come to that place where they meet themselves, others, and God. When we wait, we know and acknowledge that we are not in control.

During the time of the conciliation efforts in Nicaragua in the 1980s, I had a great deal of interaction with Tomas Borge, then minister of the interior. *Comandante* Borge was known as a brilliant and complex man. He was widely viewed by the U.S. government and his enemies as the hard-line Communist and the driving force behind a Nicaraguan and Central American threat to capitalism and freedom. Because of that, he had been deemed a threat to the U.S. national security. He was viewed by the Sandinista loyalists as one of the founders of a great liberation movement.

Borge did not profess to be a Christian. Yet once he commented to us that while he turned away from priesthood and formal religion, he had tried for years to "kill the God inside of me, but he just won't die." He spent years in jail and had been tortured extensively under the Somoza regime.

After he rose to power with the Sandinista Revolution, it was widely reported that one of his former torturers was caught. His lieutenants brought the man to his office. "Here, Comandante," they said, "here he is. You decide his fate. It is your revenge." Others reported that Borge responded, "My revenge is to forgive you."

He even wrote a book about his theology and chose a Spanish title that in translation means *Impatient Patience* (Borge). This title is much like the late-night conversations we had as we waited for negotiations to proceed, for a phone call to go through, or for a document to be redrafted once more. It captures the stance of wanting things to move ahead quickly and yet learning to wait for the time and place to be right.

Borge's book title has a biblical quality, likely influenced by the letter to the Hebrews. There the author admonishes the believers, as in the Spanish translation, "to run with patience the race that has been set before us" (Heb. 12:1; cf. KJV).

How do we run a race with patience? In my work, I believe this means learning to hold steady in the midst of chaos that swirls around us. I learned about this from fellow mediator Andy Shogreen as we pursued the conciliation efforts with Tomas Borge.

Andy was the superintendent of the Moravian Church in Nicaragua during the 1980s. He gave of himself and family perhaps as much as anyone during those years, for the sake of God's kingdom and for peace in his native country. Andy and I worked closely together during about two years, through the most intense moments of the negotiation.

In that work, Andy and I displayed different personality traits. On the outside, I may have appeared to be fairly calm, quiet, and collected. Yet inside, I often felt an emotional turmoil of monumental proportions. On the outside, Andy could easily seem to be a bit unorganized, always gregarious, and running about without much direction. Yet inside himself, he was quite clear about the progress of events and timing.

Once I became nervous about getting somewhere right on time. He commented, "You know the difference between you folks from up North and us folks down here? Well, you all have the watch, but we have the time."

I learned about waiting through an incident in the final preparation of the direct negotiation talks. We had worked for nearly two years to get both the government of Nicaragua and the Yatama Resistance leaders to agree on meeting each other face-to-face. Such talks had the potential to end the war. We had experienced many pitfalls and ups and downs.

Finally, we had a basic agreement from both sides as to when, where, and how the much-awaited event would take place. One day before the entry of a delegation of Yatama leaders into Nicaragua, Andy and I were in Borge's office making last-minute arrangements for the face-to-face meeting. I do not recall what all the reasons were, but Borge had concluded that the entry of the Yatama leaders had to be called off. We pleaded, but he said it could not be done.

We left the office. Andy told me, "He will call us this afternoon. Let's go home and wait."

I was not convinced. By the time we reached Andy's home, I was making the case that we should go back and talk to Borge. But Andy was firm: "He will call us this afternoon."

After listening to my anxious pleading one more time, Andy finally said, "Well, if that's how you feel, let's make a bet. I wager that Borge will call us by 3:00 in the afternoon."

"Okay," I said, "I will bet you a steak dinner that he does not call us by 3:00."

"A steak dinner?" Andy scoffed at me. "I mean a *real* bet! I will bet you a hundred dollars he calls us by 3:00."

"You're on!" I retorted out of pure nervousness. Then we set to waiting. I was in and out of chairs, pacing around, and wringing my fingers. Andy started working on his car as if nothing was happening.

"Two years of work!" I kept thinking. "Two years of work, and he is puttering with his car." Twelve noon came and went. One o'clock, 2:00, and then 2:30. Still we had not received a call. By then I was nearly beside myself with worry about how we were going get to Borge so late in the day, and still catch the flight back to Costa Rica to accompany the delegation into Nicaragua. Two forty-five, 2:50. Then at 2:55 the phone rang.

Andy answered. He turned my way with a hundred-dollar smile on his face. He joked, "So the minister of the interior has decided to call the minister of God." Comandante Borge was asking us to rush to the office immediately. They were ready to let the delegation come.

Over the years, I have learned about waiting from my travels. Usually I travel by airplane and have learned never to expect anything to be exactly like it was planned. Airline travel has taught me a lot. I have had more than my fair share of delayed flights and have learned about myself from them.

If a flight is delayed and they tell me when it is to depart, I wait in the airport lounge because I expect it to leave at the newly designated time. If they delay it again, I am frustrated but still wait because I still expect it to leave. If at the end of the day they cancel the flight, I am really angry and hear myself saying, "If you had told me it was not leaving today, I would not have wasted my time sitting here waiting in the lounge all day."

To wait is to expect. If we do not expect something to happen, we stop waiting. In Spanish "to wait, to expect, and to hope" are all worked into one verb, *esperar*. This is how I see the place of waiting in the journey toward reconciliation. To wait is to expect, hope, and develop patience. Paul writes what I now know more from experience than from intellect: "Who hopes for what is seen? But if we hope for what we do not see, we wait for it with patience" (Rom. 8:24-25).

Conclusion

I began this chapter with three short stories about friends and colleagues from three different places. They struggled and continue to struggle with disillusionment as they face the ups and downs of working for peace and reconciliation. I confess that in the journey toward reconciliation, disillusionment is the single greatest challenge I face.

Over the past few years, our work for reconciliation in the face of deep-rooted violent conflict has involved the teaching and mastery of technique and strategic approaches. Yet I have come to believe that a much more important aspect of this peacebuilding work is sustaining and nurturing hope. The long-term nature of working for reconciliation can raise and then dash our deepest aspirations. This places us on a path where we must regularly face a fork in the road. Disillusionment will either lead us toward despair or into a tenaciously rooted hope.

Here we can return to *wander, wonder*, and *wait* as companions for our journey. Disillusionment does not raise its head when we feel we are *far off* from making real our hopes. Disillusionment slaps us the hardest when what we have hoped for all these years has come *close*. We can see the progress. We have moved so close that we can almost touch and feel it. Then it starts to slip. We feel that we are being crushed, like dry grass trampled underfoot. We have an overwhelming sense of being tired.

Such fatigue is what I felt time and again in Nicaragua, Somalia, the Philippines, and Northern Ireland. This is what Rose, Zoilamerica, Ricardo, Joe, and Brendan have felt year in and year out, in their respective countries.

We realize that we are tired of wandering. We don't

want to wander any more. We want the trip to be over. We want to know where we are going, and we want to get there. We want to say, We have arrived at our destination. We are tired of walking. We are sick with the feeling that we are in a permanent roundabout (traffic circle), where the only road out that we can see is the road we came in on, and we know we can't go back down that one.

We want to stop wondering. We want to know for sure. We do not want the ambiguities of yet another political waffle. We hear our own voices shouting deep inside, *Enough is enough!* We want clear, concluding, and concise answers. We want solutions. We want an end that we can see, one that works and one that lasts.

We are tired of waiting. It is like sitting in an airport a long way from home, and every few hours they just keep announcing over the loudspeaker, "Your flight has been delayed." We are *so* tired of waiting! The thought that has nagged us all of our life starts to seep out uncontrolled into our minds and hearts. *Maybe what we expected will never happen. Maybe what we've been waiting for is actually not possible. We want out of this waiting room. If the plane is never going to leave, then just tell us.* We are tired of waiting!

Disillusionment presents such a fork in the road. When it moves toward despair, it is often with one of two outcomes: We either find someone to blame, or we give up. We tell ourselves it was stupid to expect it to happen.

We stop wandering because we know now that we weren't going anywhere. We stop wondering because we know now that it will never happen. If we do this, disillusionment leads to despair. Despair means giving up hope. Giving up hope means to stop waiting. We do not wait for what we do not expect. We do not wonder about things we know will not happen. We do not wander if we know we won't get there anyhow. However, we must understand that when disillusionment leads to despair, we are condemned. We are condemned to have our future defined by our past failure.

There is another side to disillusionment. We have the opportunity of embracing wandering, wondering, and waiting as yokefellows and companions on our journey rather than as enemies. With this view, we see disillusionment as necessary, as a reality check, as good for our strength and soul. It is good for our journey. We need disillusionment to build true hope.

I do not want a cheap hope. I do not want an easy way to achieve hope. I do not want a hope that can be purchased on the shelves of a supermarket. I want the real thing. I want to yearn from deep within. I want to hear the groans of creation in all its parts, as if in childbirth (Rom. 8:22-23).

I want to feel and walk alongside the coming forth of what will be, knowing that it cannot now be seen but that I hope and know it will come. To see it is no longer to hope. Who hopes for what is already seen? We hope for what we do not see, and we wait for it with patience. We run toward it with patience (Rom. 8:24-25; Heb. 11:1; 12:1).

We know where the train of history is going. We just can't see the destination quite yet. It is *a dream*, a hope that we keep alive. We need the disillusionment to remind us that we are yet wandering, wondering, and waiting, but we know it is coming. This is a time of great disillusionment in many places. Let it come. Let it come. For now is a time for great hope.

14
THE DREAM

As I write these words, we are near the end of the twentieth century, living in a period of fast changes, at the close of a decade that gave us great promise, challenge, and pain. We started this decade with the promise of peace.

In Berlin we saw, metaphorically and physically, the walls of hostility crumble before our eyes. "Is the dream of peace actually possible?" we asked. There was a sense of promise and celebration. We could all feel the words of the poet stirring within us: "Something there is that doesn't love a wall" (Robert Frost, "Mending Wall"). *Maybe peace is not a utopian dream,* we thought.

Within a year we experienced the unleashing of the Gulf War. Flashing across our televisions and newspapers, we stood, almost dumbfounded, as the death machine with its modern flamboyance, sheer power, and advanced technology captured our unbelieving eyes and imagination. "What happened to the dream of peace?" we managed to stutter to each other, our voices drowned out in the din of war-making. We heard cries for victory and support for our troops in atonement for past failures. We fell almost deathly silent, our dream of peace unreal and invalidated.

Then we watched untold atrocities in Somalia, Rwanda, and the former Yugoslavia that have numbed our senses and left us in the international community feeling paralyzed. These are difficult times for dreams.

For some time I have been interested in this human activity known as dreaming. My first encounter with dreaming at an explicit level came in the form of a question put to me: "What do you want to be when you grow up?" I found this question more annoying as I grew older. But as a child, it was exciting and filled with so many options. We faced the question with the innocence of wide eyes and unlimited ideas. Everything and anything was possible.

In my family the story is told of my first answer to that query. Apparently some well-meaning adults raised this question of future vocation and identity before a few friends and me. One friend quickly said, "A fireman." A second responded, "A doctor." And then I said, with the highest of aspirations, "I want to be a football."

The process of "growing up" and "becoming mature" shifts us out of childhood dreaming, out of innocence about the possible, and delivers us into the realities of adulthood. *Growing up* seems to mean "getting realistic." We are asked to become a part of the real world. But I am worried about what we lose in this process. To put it bluntly, I am worried about the extinction of a particular human species: *the Dreamer.*

We seem to have a scarcity of dreamers these days. I often cite the words of Langston Hughes. In several of his poems, he voiced a similar concern. "The Dream Keeper" calls us to bring all of our dreams, so they can be protected from the "too-rough fingers of the world." In "Dreams," the author advises us to "hold fast to dreams," for without them life is "frozen" and "barren," grounded like "a broken-winged bird" (Hughes).

Dreaming has to do with the simple act of connecting

the present and the future. I have noticed at least two different ways of relating the present and the future. The first we could identify as futurologists, from people like palm readers and stockbrokers to specialists like Alvin Toffler and John Naisbeth. They tackle dreaming by reading the signs and the times and then predicting where we will be in the future. In simple words, they look at what is and suggest what will be, based on those realities. This is what we call *realism.*

In one form or another, we all engage in understanding how things work and what is likely to happen in the future. This is a needed and useful endeavor in many circumstances. We can plan and prepare for our education, for our jobs, and for our children's future.

Among other things, I am an educator. In education, we are intentional about trying to understand how the world is made up and how it functions, from its physics to its sociology. Education is a set of lenses that permits us to look at our world and ourselves with care and objectivity.

My training is that of a sociologist and a mediator. With careful and open eyes, I apply the lenses of my training to the condition of our human family. What I see is both challenging and overwhelming. The realities around us are harsh. On the planet Earth, we are living amid a humanity filled with need. Look for a moment through a few windows into this house we humans call home. Observe how we have chosen to organize ourselves in the real world.

This decade began with the opening of the Gulf War. Seven years later we stand on the verge of a second round of war-plane fire. In the Gulf War, we as a nation brought our national resources to bear in an unprecedented effort to militarily liberate a country inhabited by a few million people. Yet we have never channeled such effort or resource toward alleviating basic human need, at home or abroad.

The billions spent in the first months of the war would have funded the current annual budget of the World Food Program of the UN for the next two hundred years. We spent more in research and deployment of the first ten bombing sorties across Iraq than we will likely spend as a nation in this decade to house the homeless in our major cities. That is the reality of our world.

When we look closer, the situation seems worse. A bird's-eye view tells us a much broader and more disturbing story. Across the world, there are more than forty armed conflicts, *forty wars* being fought as I write these words. There is a geography to these wars. The vast majority are carried out in the Southern Hemisphere, in countries already hopelessly burdened with poverty, starvation, poor health services, and overwhelming national debts.

Many of the forty are internal wars, often fought over issues of identity, ethnicity, and religion. They are long-term, protracted conflicts; some have lasted for more than forty years. Recent UN reports indicate that in the past ten years, refugee populations across the globe increased from seven million to more than seventeen million (Lederach: *Building Peace*).

That is the reality of our world today. If nothing else, these windows looking into the condition of our planet tell us that we live in a violent world. Its resources are not shared equally and not developed to meet basic human needs. Racism and fear still run strong. Health, education, and housing sit at the bottom of national and world priorities. Human conflict is resolved by whoever carries the biggest stick. When we look realistically at our world, these are the challenges we face.

However, we must be careful with our embrace of objective knowledge and realism, for both involve a subtle premise. Realism assumes that *what is now* and *what must be in the future* are the same. Tomorrow is seen as the slave of today. Too often we find ourselves succumbing and adapting to the way things are. Too often "getting realistic" means "fitting in" and "going along." We adapt and give up our dreams to fit the way things are in the real world.

Thus our desire to be realistic pulls us toward looking with objective and descriptive eyes at what is around us. It keeps our feet grounded in the practical challenges we face. But we must not permit ourselves to be defined by the realities those challenges represent. Understanding the realities in which we live must not translate into a simple acceptance that *this* is the way things should be.

Biblical Dreamers

The Bible story presents a second approach to dreaming. In many ways, Scripture is a big anthology of dreams and dreamers. For me, this is summed up in a single verse that describes faith, as written to the Hebrews. "Faith is the assurance of things hoped for, the conviction of things not seen" (Heb. 11:1). As one translation puts it, "Faith makes us certain of realities we do not see" (NEB).

Apparently this author did not want people lost in the abstractness of the statement. To make the practical essence of this affirmation clear, we are given about forty more verses laying out a long list of illustrative case examples. These are people who lived according to unseen realities.

For examples, crazy Noah built a boat to prepare for a flood when it was as dry as a bone. Wandering Abraham left his home to receive his inheritance without even knowing where he was going. Spunky Sarah continued to act like she was going to have a baby even though she was far past the usual childbearing age.

These models of faith, these people, these biblical dreamers—these are known as the *cloud*, the "cloud of witnesses" (Heb. 12:1). Their dreaming did not predict the future according to the present. Instead, quite the opposite is true. They changed present reality by living according to a vision of the future. We are told that this is "faith" (11:39). These people did not live by the way things are but according to a vision of things not seen. That vision of things not seen eventually changes the way things are.

Clarence Jordan once translated this verse as saying, "Faith is turning dreams into deeds." Proverbs tells us, "Where there is no vision, the people perish" (Prov. 29:18, KJV). To put it bluntly, "Dream or die!" This is not a literal death, but it is a death of accepting and accommodating to the way things are, instead of living as if they could be different.

I am reminded of close friends in Nicaragua. We held a workshop with some key leaders in local and regional peace commissions originally formed under the Central American peace plan. During our time together, my friends started telling stories of their mediation work. One was Pedrito.

Though Pedrito had little formal education, he was an elected leader of a cooperative movement representing more than two thousand campesinos. He talked about the complications and difficulties of traveling by foot or horseback more than five days into the mountains. He was seeking out people who were still armed. He would build bridges with them and encourage them to come down and meet their enemies face-to-face. Then he trekked five days back by foot to meet with the government and army officials and encourage them to meet leaders of these opposition forces.

I asked my friends why they took on these dangerous tasks. Pedrito simply answered, "We all want peace. We, we who are bearers of the good news, have been given the ministry of reconciliation. It is our job, our responsibility."

That afternoon we lunched in the hot Managua sun. Pedrito had asked the maintenance people at the hotel for a sack. He was filling it with big seed pods that were falling on the veranda from a huge Guanacaste tree overhead. I asked him what he was doing, and he said, "We have a problem with deforestation in my area. I want to take back these seeds for the people. Nobody here really seems to want them."

I will remember the image of Pedrito walking toward his bus stop with his huge white sack of Guanacaste seeds on his back. This was a symbolic sack of dreams for his people. It embodied the ministry of reconciliation that not only bridges human conflict but cares and gives back to the creation what God has provided. The harvest of justice, we are told, is sown in peace by those who make peace (cf. James 3:18, NEB).

Pedrito is a dreamer. He has his feet grounded in the realities of his native Nicaragua and his head in the clouds. Day in and out, he is living by a dream that things can be different. Each of us needs our own big sack of Guanacaste seeds, our sack of dreams that we carry on our way.

The journey toward reconciliation calls us to embrace the paradox. Caught as we are between the realities we see around us and the dreams we have, we must not choose one over the other. To move toward reconciliation, we must keep our feet on the ground, connected to the pulse of real-life challenges, and our heads in the cloud, with a dream that things can be different.

In Colombia they have a saying, "You must be so close to the ground that you can hear the grass grow." This is our challenge: To stay so close to the ground that we feel the very soil's moisture bubbling up from people's daily life, pains, and realities. Yet we must be so close to our dreams of what could be that we can feel and hear the seeds pregnant with life as they break forth from below the surface.

Faith beckons us to join the cloud of witnesses. We are invited to join people having a practical commitment to face the challenges of their day, and simultaneously the courage to dream about what could and should be.

Twenty-five years ago, the voice of Martin Luther King Jr. thundered across our nation's capital with the simple words "I have a dream." That speech stands out, not only for his call to racial equality and justice, but for his simple audacity to dream at a time like his.

At the outbreak of the Gulf War, I went back to an old book by Harry Emerson Fosdick, with sermons preached during World War II (Fosdick). I was interested in these sermons in part because I had always been inspired by the words of his hymn "God of Grace and God of Glory." I wanted to hear what God was saying through this servant in wartime. His words leapt out from the first pages, surpassing the dimension of time and context:

So let Christianity speak in an era like this! Our problem is not to see how little we can believe but what great things we can see in the Christian message and make real to the world that desperately needs them. This is a great time for great convictions.

Sam Doe's Dream

For the past few years, I have had the great privilege of working, teaching, and learning from Sam Doe. Sam is from Liberia, where he has toiled the ground of peacebuilding during the many long years of ethnic fighting and violence. As part of our master's program at Eastern Mennonite University, he told the story of how he came to work with child soldiers that have been so common in the Liberian war.

Sam initiated a number of workshops with the Christian Health Association of Liberia. They began to work with young children who had been fighters for one faction or other in the war. Sam tells of one young man by the name of Korte. He had been taken at a young age into the ranks of the fighters. When they were inducted at ages nine to twelve, they were often sent back into the very areas and villages they came from, with a mission to destroy everything that was there.

The warlords assigned the boys to commit such atrocious acts to create loyalty in their hearts and minds. Afterward, the boys attached their security, lives, and futures to the local militias. At age ten, Korte was changed in such a way.

When Sam met him, he was in a refugee encampment and experiencing hallucinations from his recent violent experiences and the steady flow of drugs he had been fed. Sam worked with him day in and day out. Korte would have visual and aural visions that pushed him to violence. He would say that his grandmother was calling him to do these things. Sam told him that whenever Korte had a vision, he should come to Sam. On numerous occasions, Sam had to deal with violent confrontations and bring Korte back to real life.

One day, however, Sam needed to leave for a week in neighboring Ivory Coast. When he returned a week later, his colleagues told him that Korte was dead. Just a few days earlier, he had come to the office with bad hallucinations. Claiming that he was a prince, the son of the King of the Coast, he said his father was calling him home. Within a few hours, he had walked into the salty tide of a nearby beach and drowned. At sixteen, after carrying a gun in a war of adults for six years, Korte was dead.

Sam was devastated. He recalls going straight home from the office. After a few hours at home, he walked out to the beach where only days before Korte had committed suicide. There Sam found himself struggling with a deep sense of anger and despair. At first he was angry with his colleagues. "Why," he heard himself nearly shouting at them as if they were there, "did you not do something to stop him?"

He was also angry at himself. "Why did I even go to Ivory Coast? Why didn't I stay home?"

Then he found himself addressing God. "Why did you create a small boy and let him fall into the hands of such violence and evil? Where were you when Korte needed you most?"

Sam says he waded for hours along the shore, between tears of sadness and tears of anger. After that long afternoon, he arose with a new conviction, one that would carry him through his next hours and days, years, and a lifetime. "I will give my life to working with child soldiers, making sure this madness of violence does not destroy our country."

From the first time I met Sam, he has always talked about his dream, the dream that one day justice, peace, and reconciliation would root themselves and grow in Liberia. As I write these words, Sam is traveling in West Africa and in his native Liberia, giving seminars on peacebuilding, trauma healing, and working with child soldiers. That day at the beach, the seeds of a dream were born from the waters of despair and harsh reality.

Sam has his feet deep in his native soil, a soil drenched with too much blood and suffering. He has his head in the clouds, believing so firmly that reconciliation is possible that he has chosen to give his whole lifework to make it come true.

Are we not all faced with the same questions that face Sam? What dreams do we people of faith have? Is not the dream of reconciliation a real possibility, where all things are brought together? Cannot our dreams and convictions have the power of transformation in the face of today's real challenges? Are these not the dreams of our Creator? What kind of God do we believe in?

Believing and Dreaming

I believe in the God of history, the God of creation, the God of love and compassion, the God of immeasurable power. This God has chosen to work through the weak and foolish. To rescue enemies, this God chose to give away a child, the beloved Son, the one most cherished (see chapter 2).

I believe in a God who, like a mother or a father, sees and cares for each child on this earth through the eyes of a parent and not through the eyes of nationality. This parent weeps at the pain and death that some children inflict on others.

I believe in the God of Shalom, who invites us to be a part of the new kingdom dream. There human energies are spent on healing the sick, housing the homeless, and feeding the hungry. There we choose not the weapons of destruction to resolve our differences but the God-given gifts of reason and speech, and the overwhelming coals of love and compassion (cf. Rom. 12:20).

I believe justice, peace, and reconciliation are possible. I believe they will happen.

I believe that some years hence, Liberia, that small West African country, will receive an international award for their groundbreaking educational programs with youth. When the minister of education receives the reward, he will give credit to his great-grandfather, who was a child-soldier in the war that broke the country. But he was lifted from the bitter cycles of violent hopelessness and self-destruction by the work of the revered peacemakers Sam Doe and Marion Subah.

"They lived," he will say, "in such a way that it inspired a dream in my grandfather for educating children, a dream that has been passed on to us today. We accept this award," he will say, "to fulfill the dream of a child-soldier that the day will come when no children in Africa will suffer the violence of the gun."

I believe that someday the president of the United States will, with a single stroke of her pen, sign a bill that dismantles the Department of Defense, the Pentagon, and the CIA. In her closing speech, she will refer to her great-grandparents' dream, born from an encounter in a Summer Peacebuilding Institute in the Shenandoah

Valley many years earlier.

"Today," she will say, and I can hear these words tumbling from the television sets, "we are taking a step to realize the dream that we need to create a world where our security lies in the quality of our relationships, not the quantity of our weapons."

I believe the day will come when the children of Joe and Janet Campbell and Brendan and Elizabeth McAllister will hold their own grandchildren on their laps by the glow of a coal fire on a wintry Irish eve. To postpone going to bed, the grandchildren will beg for a story: "Grandmom, Granddad, tell us again. How did the troubles end?"

These are the dreams. But make no mistake! It takes courage and tenacity to dream in times like these. We are faced with a world of broken people, a world of violence and war, inequality and injustice, a world of famine and poverty. We are not blocked or restrained by a lack of resources for responding to these problems. We are shackled by a lack of imagination and dreaming that things can be otherwise, by a lack of commitment to live by those dreams with the conviction that they are possible.

So let me close with the encouragement of the letter to the Hebrews. To take up the journey of reconciliation, we keep our feet on the ground and our head in the clouds. Now is the time for great convictions and great dreams. Let us dream boldly. Let us dream boldly that our feet may carry us through the challenging realities that stir around us.

May God grant us the innocence to dream, and the wisdom, courage, and sustenance to take up the journey.

BIBLIOGRAPHY

Achebe, Chinua. *Things Fall Apart.* Oxford: Heinemann International Publishing, 1988.

Borge, Tomas. *Christianity and Revolution: Tomas Borge's Theology of Life.* Trans. Andrew Reading. New York: Orbis Books, 1987.

Chandler, David. *Brother Number One: A Political Biography of Pol Pot.* Boulder, Colo.: Westview Press, 1992.

Fosdick, Harry Emerson. *A Great Time to Be Alive: Sermons on Christianity in Wartime.* New York: Harper and Brothers, 1944.

Friedman, Edwin H. *Generation to Generation.* New York: Guilford Press, 1985.

Gandhi, Mahatma. *An Autobiography, Or, The Story of My Experiments with Truth.* Ahmedabad, India: The Navajivan Press, 1976.

George, K. M. *The Silent Roots.* Geneva: WCC Publications, 1994.

Hall, Edward T. *The Dance of Life.* New York: Anchor Books, 1984.

Heinrich, Wolfgang. *Building the Peace.* Uppsala, Sweden: Life and Peace Institute, 1997.

Hocker, Joyce, and William Wilmot. *Interpersonal Conflict.* Dubuque, Iowa: Brown and Benchmark Publishers, 1995.

Hughes, Langston. "The Dream Keeper." "Dreams." In *The Dream Keeper and Other Poems.* New York: Alfred A. Knopf Books for Young Readers, 1994.

Kraybill, Ron. *Repairing the Breach.* Scottdale, Pa.: Herald Press, 1981.

Laue, Jim, and Gerald Cormick. "The Ethics of Intervention in

Community Disputes." In *The Ethics of Social Intervention.* Ed. Gordan Bermat, Herbert Kelman, and Donald Warwick. Washington, D.C.: Halsted Press, 1979.

Lederach, John Paul. *Building Peace: Sustainable Reconciliation in Divided Societies.* Washington, D.C.: United States Institute of Peace Press, 1997.

_____. *Preparing for Peace: Conflict Transformation Across Cultures.* Syracuse: Syracuse Univ. Press, 1996.

_____. *See also* Sampson and Lederach

Lehman, F. M. "The Love of God." No. 538 in *The Mennonite Hymnal.* Scottdale, Pa.: Herald Press, 1969.

Mennonite Conciliation Service. *Mediation and Facilitation Training Manual.* Akron, Pa.: Mennonite Central Committee, 1995.

Muller-Fahrenholz, Geiko. *The Art of Forgiveness.* Geneva: WCC Publications, 1997.

Sampson, Cynthia, and John Paul Lederach, eds. "From the Ground Up: Mennonite Contributions to International Peacebuilding." Manuscript written with grant from the United States Institute of Peace, 1997.

Watzlawick, P., J. Weakland, and Richard Fisch. *Change.* New York: W. W. Norton, 1978.

Wehr, Paul. *Conflict Regulation.* Boulder, Colo.: Westview Press, 1979.

Wink, Walter. *When the Powers Fall: Reconciliation in the Healing of Nations.* Minneapolis: Augsburg Fortress, 1998.

THE AUTHOR

John Paul Lederach has worked in international conciliation for more than twenty years. He has been developing training in conflict transformation and providing
direct mediation and support services for reconciliation
efforts in some of the most violently conflicted regions
across five continents.

Lederach has consulted with the highest-level government officials and national opposition movements in
war-torn settings like Nicaragua, Somalia, Northern Ire-

Angie, Wendy, John Paul, and Josh Lederach

land, the Basque Provinces, and the Philippines. His service includes interpersonal, family, organizational, church, and community mediation.

He is the founding director of the Conflict Transformation Program at Eastern Mennonite University, Harrisonburg, Virginia, where he teaches both undergraduate and graduate courses. He is the former director of the Mennonite Conciliation Service and the International Conciliation Service of the Mennonite Central Committee.

Lederach is the author of eleven books and manuals, and numerous academic articles and monographs on peace education, conflict transformation, and mediation training. He is in international demand as a lecturer, consultant, and mediation trainer.

John Paul Lederach was born in Indiana but grew up in Oregon and Kansas. He has lived outside the United States in Belgium, Spain, and Costa Rica. He is married to Wendy S. Liechty. They are the parents of Angie and Josh and attend Community Mennonite Church in Harrisonburg.